Trade and Gender Review of New Zealand

Please cite this publication as:
OECD (2022), *Trade and Gender Review of New Zealand*, OECD Publishing, Paris, https://doi.org/10.1787/923576ea-en.

ISBN 978-92-64-57030-6 (print)
ISBN 978-92-64-78681-3 (pdf)
ISBN 978-92-64-65132-6 (HTML)
ISBN 978-92-64-54560-1 (epub)

Photo credits: Cover © iStock.com/Avishai Futerman.

Corrigenda to publications may be found on line at: www.oecd.org/about/publishing/corrigenda.htm.

Foreword

This OECD *Trade and Gender Review* sheds light on the impacts of trade and trade policies on New Zealand women as workers, consumers, and business owners and leaders. This review is informed by New Zealand's Trade for All Agenda and draws on the OECD's Trade and Gender Framework of Analysis. It sets out a number of policy recommendations to ensure New Zealand women share in the benefits from trade.

This *Review* is a joint project between the New Zealand Ministry of Foreign Affairs and Trade (MFAT) and the Trade and Agriculture Directorate (TAD) of the OECD. The research and analysis undertaken by OECD employed and adapted in-house tools such as the Services Trade Restrictiveness Index (STRI), the Trade Facilitation Indicators (TFI), and the METRO trade model. The *Review* benefitted from recently developed gender-disaggregated trade data from New Zealand's administrative and other datasets by the Economic Division of MFAT. Quantitative findings were complemented by qualitative input gathered during a series of workshops and interviews with women entrepreneurs and exporters. Recommendations on policy settings were developed by the OECD in consultation with officials from a range of New Zealand government agencies.

The evidence and policy recommendations presented in this *Review* aim to inform future actions by New Zealand to improve women's participation in trade. It is also hoped that this *Review* can serve as a template for similar trade and gender reviews of other countries.

Acknowledgements

The lead authors of this *Review* were Jane Korinek of the OECD and Phil Mellor of the New Zealand Ministry of Foreign Affairs and Trade (MFAT). Other contributing authors were Christine Arriola, Sebastian Benz and Silvia Sorescu of the OECD; Chris Brunt, Neil Cribbens and Sam Verevis of MFAT; and Caroline Dommen, independent consultant. Ana-Maria Muresan provided statistical assistance, and Laëtitia Christophe and Michèle Patterson provided editorial assistance.

The research benefitted from substantive comments and discussions in the OECD Working Party of the Trade Committee.

The authors would like to thank New Zealand government officials for their co-operation and insights, in particular Rebecca Barnes and Anna Macdonald of the Ministry for Women, Jordan Allison, Gaia Church, Charlotte Frater, Ed McIsaac and James Messent of the Ministry of Foreign Affairs and Trade, Saba Vallipuram of the New Zealand Customs Service, and Anna Guenther, Anna Ruediger and the wider team at New Zealand Trade and Enterprise.

The authors are grateful to John Drummond, Julia Nielson, and Marion Jansen of the OECD for their guidance and insightful comments.

Finally, the authors would like to thank Chantelle Cole, Stephanie Honey, Desi Lorand, Annabelle O'Donnell, Tara Pradhan and Rachel Taulelei for generously sharing their experiences on entrepreneurship and exporting from New Zealand.

Table of contents

FIGURES

TABLES

Executive Summary

The OECD Trade and Gender Framework of Analysis establishes an approach to understanding the impact of international trade and trade policies on women in three key economic roles: as workers, as consumers and as business owners and leaders. This *Trade and Gender Review of New Zealand*, undertaken jointly by the OECD and the New Zealand Ministry of Foreign Affairs and Trade (MFAT), employs quantitative and qualitative analysis to identify policy steps towards ensuring that that open markets and a rules-based international trading system in good working order contribute to women's economic empowerment.

Women as workers: From the perspective of women as workers, the Review demonstrates that, although women's participation in trade-related jobs has grown, and grown faster than that of their male counterparts, women remain underrepresented in trade-related jobs. Today, women comprise about 40% of New Zealand's export-related employment. While women are more engaged in exporting than ever before, they remain underrepresented in export employment compared to their share of the total workforce, where they make up 47% of persons employed, and the working age population, of which they comprise 51%. Moreover, women's participation in export sectors, although having grown significantly, has grown less than their participation in non-export sectors.

Women as entrepreneurs and business leaders: Similar to women workers, women entrepreneurs and business leaders are less engaged in trade than their male counterparts. This is in part due to the smaller size of their businesses; small firms tend to be less engaged in trade than larger firms. That said, women-led firms have a marginally higher export propensity than men-owned firms of similar size. So while women appear to be significantly less likely to lead a firm (including an export firm) and their firms are generally smaller, those firms that they do lead are marginally more willing to sell overseas compared to similar sized firms led by their male counterparts.

Women as consumers: One of the main gains from trade is to lower prices and increase the purchasing power of women consumers. Since lower-income households tend to spend a larger share of their income, rather than saving or investing, their purchasing power rises more when trade barriers are reduced and consumer prices fall. A stylized scenario of an increase in New Zealand tariff rates on imported goods from all countries except Australia to 25% estimated a drop in purchasing power parity of 9% in more vulnerable household types, such as single-parent households with dependent children. Women lead the vast majority of these households. These findings indicate that more vulnerable household types tend to benefit from lower consumer prices that are brought on by trade even more than less vulnerable household types, such as those with more than one adult.

Main findings

New Zealand is a small, open economy that ranks highly globally in terms of its trade policies, both in terms of it policies at the border and those that facilitate trade. New Zealand is ranked fourth globally out of 180 countries in terms of gender equality according to the World Economic Forum (2021[1]). Building on existing policies, the following trade and gender policy steps can help to ensure that open markets and a rules-based international trading system in good working order contribute to women's economic empowerment.

- *Making trade agreements more gender-sensitive*: *Ex ante* impact assessments, the optimization of existing gender-related provisions, new or revised gender-responsive provisions, and strengthened monitoring and institutional support can make New Zealand's trade agreements more gender-sensitive.
- *Support for gender-sensitive policymaking in plurilateral contexts:* New Zealand could support and promote gender-responsive policy initiatives such as the Global Trade and Gender Arrangement (GTAGA), application of the non-discrimination clause in the WTO Reference Paper on Services Domestic Regulation, ongoing work in APEC and elsewhere on gender-responsive standards, and the ongoing initiatives in WTO on trade and gender.
- *Communication of the benefits of trade agreements*: SMEs are less aware and less able to take advantage of the opportunities under trade agreements. Efforts to ensure that the benefits of trade deals are more widely understood, in particular by potential women exporters who may have more shallow networks, should be undertaken. Increasing public understanding of the benefits of trade and trade agreements more widely can also help to create constituencies that support open markets.
- *Market access*: New Zealand could prioritise market access reforms that would particularly benefit women. Although New Zealand is generally an open economy, there are areas, particularly in services, that could be considered for further market opening, including in relation to movement of people. Lower income consumers, where women are disproportionately found, spend more of their income and benefit more from the lower prices that result from trade.
- *Aid for Trade*: Outside New Zealand, gender gaps are generally greater and women often face substantial legal and administrative barriers to their participation in economic activity, in addition to strongly gendered cultural norms. Thus far, women's economic empowerment has not been a stated objective in New Zealand's Aid for Trade strategy. New Zealand could consider leveraging Aid for Trade to contribute to more gender equal outcomes by mainstreaming gender in its Aid for Trade strategy.
- *Trade facilitation:* Women-owned and women-led businesses in New Zealand, as in other OECD countries, tend to be smaller than those led by men. Administrative processes that are costly, time consuming, and non-transparent increase trade costs of small firms more than large ones that have more resources to better navigate challenging business environments. Facilitating trade through simpler processes and more transparent procedures will increase small businesses' propensity to export, and decrease their trade costs. Although New Zealand ranks well among OECD countries in terms of facilitating trade, a more focused gender lens could be applied in order to ensure inclusivity in policy formulation and feedback from those impacted by facilitating measures.
- *Representation of women*: Ensuring that women are engaged in trade policymaking both as senior policy makers and as stakeholders will go a long way to ensuring trade policies work for women. A first step requires monitoring their involvement at all levels of policymaking.
- *Trade promotion*: Export promotion has been prioritised in New Zealand, both in terms of resources devoted to it, and the services the trade promotion authority, NZTE, provides. These programmes and services could be leveraged to ensure women entrepreneurs and exporters are fully supported in their export journeys.
- *Professional and business networks*: Women generally have shallower business networks (Korinek, Moïsé and Tange, 2021[2]) and seem to benefit less from traditional business networks (International Trade Centre, 2019[3]) than men. Although not strictly within the purview of government, some suggestions that aim to augment the usefulness of professional and business networks for women are included here.

- *Address data gaps*: This *Review* combines different data sources and extracts as much gender-differentiated information as possible from existing sources. Increasing collection of gender-differentiated data is one of the stated mandates both of the OECD 2021 Ministerial Council Statement[1] and the Joint Ministerial Declaration on the Advancement of Gender Equality and Women's Economic Empowerment within Trade[2] and some additional suggestions for expanding or updating some major data sources are provided.
- *Domestic policies*: Although the focus of this *Review's* policy recommendations is in the area of trade policy and its implementation, a certain number of domestic policy areas could be prioritised to ensure that women are in a position to take full advantage of the benefits of trade. These include, for example, policies that aim to close gender wage gaps, lowering the burden of unpaid work on women, ensuring representation of women in senior positions and ensuring women-led firms have equal access to government procurement contracts.

Notes

[1] "We call upon the OECD to model best practices in gender mainstreaming throughout its work, including through disaggregated data collection and analysis" (OECD 2021 Ministerial Council Statement, https://www.oecd.org/mcm/MCM-2021-Part-2-Final-Statement.EN.pdf, 5-6 October).

[2] The first of four objectives of the Joint Statement is to: "Continue to review, develop and improve national and/or regional collection of gender-disaggregated data that is comparable to the extent possible and analysis on trade and gender, to provide the basis for informed gender-responsive policies" (WTO/MIN(21)/4/Rev.1).

1. Women workers, business leaders and consumers in New Zealand

Chapter 1 examines how trade impacts women in three of their economic roles – as workers, entrepreneurs and business leaders, and consumers. It draws on new data sets, and combines data in new ways to shed light on how women engage in trade, how they are most affected by changes in consumer prices due to trade, and gender gaps in wages and entrepreneurship in export sectors. Barriers to women's participation in employment and trade, such as the distribution of unpaid work and differences in access to finance, are outlined. To the extent possible, analysis is extended to examine trade's impact on women of different ethnicities.

Women workers

Methodology and data

This chapter focusses on women's participation in trade as employees, with a focus on employment and wages. The analysis in this section uses two main approaches. The first approach is a top-down methodology that utilises the export propensity by industry from New Zealand's input-output tables to estimate export and tradables sector employment (Baily and Ford, 2018[1]). This methodology has been extended to provide gender-differentiated estimates. While straightforward to calculate and timely, this approach requires some key simplifying assumptions, the most notable of which is that the export propensity applies evenly across an industry.

The second approach is a bottom-up methodology utilising New Zealand's administrative data sets, the Longitudinal Business Database (LBD) and the Integrated Data Infrastructure (IDI). The LBD and IDI collate administrative and other data from a wide range of sources.[1,2] The LBD captures data about individual firms. Critically, customs data on goods exports and imports can be linked to individual firms. The IDI captures information about individuals (which are carefully anonymised to preserve privacy). Finally, firm data in the LBD can be linked to each firm's employee data in the IDI via monthly payroll tax filings.

Linking all this data provides a fairly comprehensive picture on whether firms participate in goods exporting activities, the characteristics of their business owners and leaders (including their gender), and their employees (the number of them, and their gender and pay characteristics). The notable gap in the data set are firms that export and import services. At present, there is no administrative data source that comprehensively measures services exports and imports. All firm-level data presented relate to the year ending March 2018 (Figure 1.1).

Figure 1.1. New Zealand administrative data subsets used for firm-level analysis

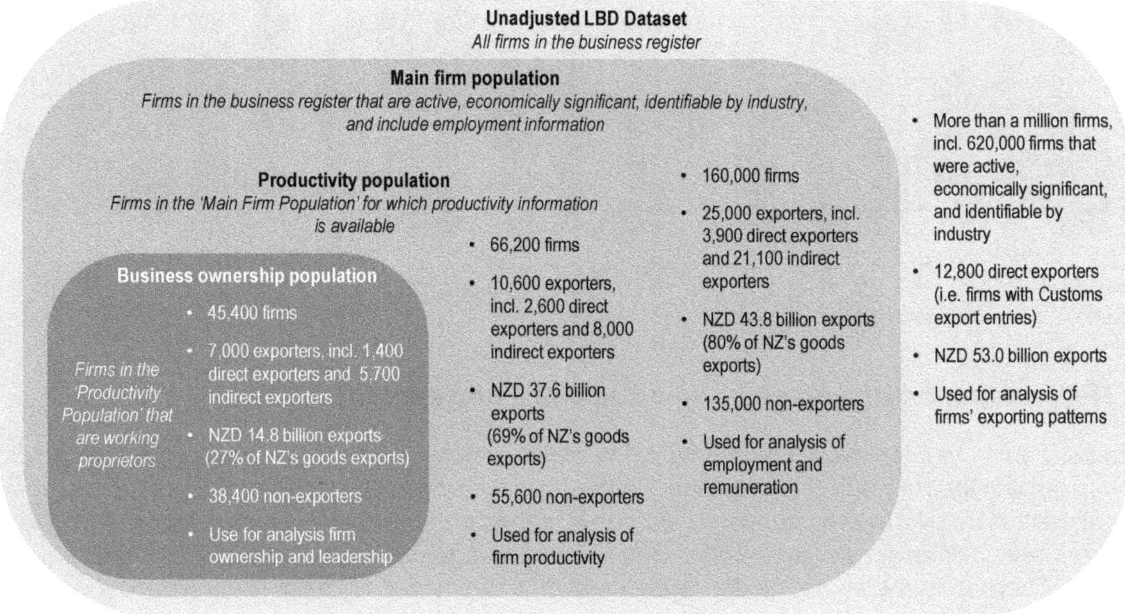

Employment of women in New Zealand's export and tradable sectors

The number of women in New Zealand who produce goods and services for export has increased steadily over the past two decades. Since 2005, women's export employment has grown by 22% to 254 000 (Figure 1.2). This outpaced growth in the number of men in export-related employment, which grew 15% to 387 000.

Over the same period, the number of women in the wider tradable sector has also increased. Women's tradable employment increased by 22% to over 510 000, compared with growth in men's tradable employment of 16%. The wider tradable sector includes employees producing goods and services for export (directly and indirectly), as well as those in industries where international competition is material enough to affect market conditions regardless of whether any individual firm has a solely domestic focus.

This has seen the proportion of jobs held by women in the export and tradable sectors lift slightly over the past two decades. The share of women's employment in the export sector increased from 38.3% to 39.6% between 2005 and 2021. The results from the firm level (goods-only export) data show a similar employment share of 40.1% in 2018. While at its highest level since data began, women remain underrepresented in export employment compared to their share of the total workforce, where they make up 47.1% of persons employed, and the working age population, where they make up 50.7%.

Figure 1.2. Export employment by gender

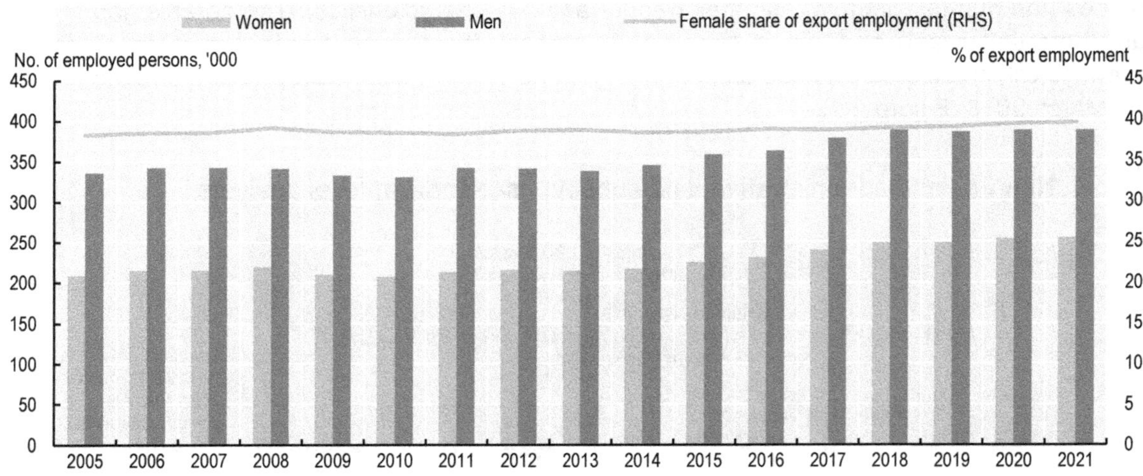

Note: Years to June quarter.
Source: Stats NZ, MFAT calculations (2021).

Representation of women in New Zealand's key exporting industries

A key factor behind women's low representation in export employment is the nature of the occupations that tend to be held by women in New Zealand. Studies of New Zealand's occupational gender segregation have found persistent over-representation of women in 'caring professions' (such as nursing, teaching and social work), administrative and sales roles, and lower-skilled service jobs (such as personal care and hospitality).[3] There is long-standing under-representation of women in farming, lower-skilled manual jobs (such as labouring and machine operating), and technical professions (such as engineering and information technology).

Given New Zealand's exports are heavily concentrated in the primary industries and related manufacturing, these occupational differences contribute to significantly lower representation of women in New Zealand's key exporting industries (Figure 1.3 and Figure 1.4). In 2020, the manufacturing, mining, and agriculture, forestry and fishing industries accounted for roughly three-quarters of New Zealand's total exports, but only a third of all export-related employment of women (compared with half of export employment of men).

Figure 1.3. Gender shares of total industry employment, 2021

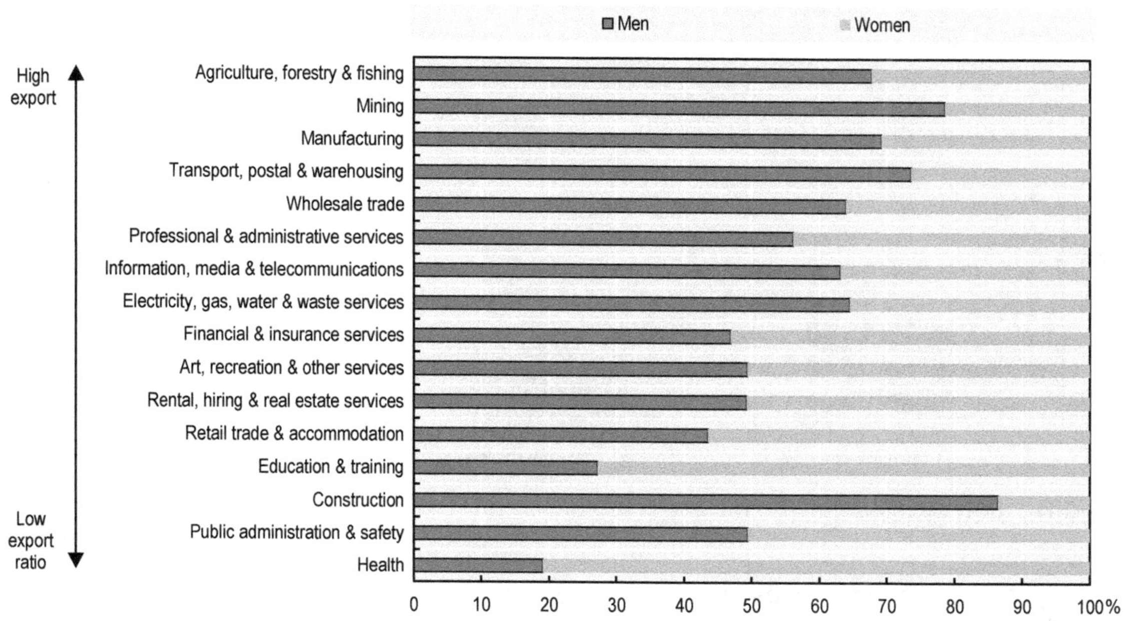

Men
Women
High export
Low export ratio
Agriculture, forestry & fishing
Mining
Manufacturing
Transport, postal & warehousing
Wholesale trade
Professional & administrative services
Information, media & telecommunications
Electricity, gas, water & waste services
Financial & insurance services
Art, recreation & other services
Rental, hiring & real estate services
Retail trade & accommodation
Education & training
Construction
Public administration & safety
Health
0
10
20
30
40
50
60
70
80
90
100%

Note: Employment data refer to shares that are based on total employment, i.e. export and non-export employment, for each industry. The ranking from high to low export intensity is based on the export ratio from input-output tables, and includes services exports.
Source: Stats NZ, MFAT calculations (2021).

Figure 1.4. Export employment by gender and industry, 2021

Men
Women
No. of persons employed, '100
100
90
80
70
60
50
40
30
20
10
0
Manufacturing
Agriculture, forestry & fishing
Professional & administrative services
Retail trade and accommodation
Transport, postal & warehousing
Art, recreation & other services
Wholesale trade
Education & training
Financial insurance services
Construction
Rental, hiring & real estate services
Information, media & telecommunications
Public administration & safety
Electricity, gas, water & waste services
Health
Mining

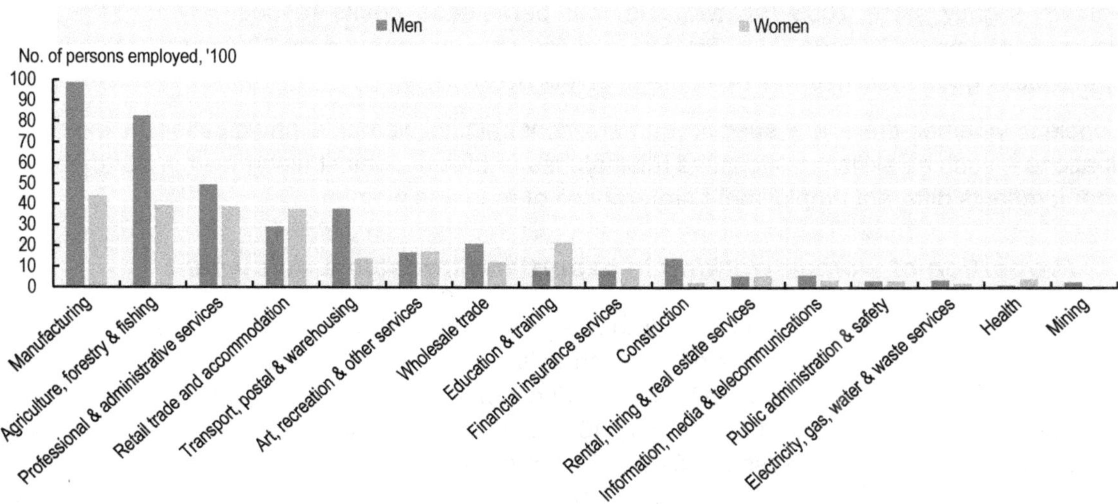

Source: Stats NZ, MFAT calculations (2021).

Firm level data for goods-only exporting paints a similar story. The firm level data also suggests that women employees are better represented in exporting sectors in larger firms (i.e. those with more than 250 staff) than they are in small firms (Figure 1.5).

Figure 1.5. Employees of exporting firms by firm size, 2018

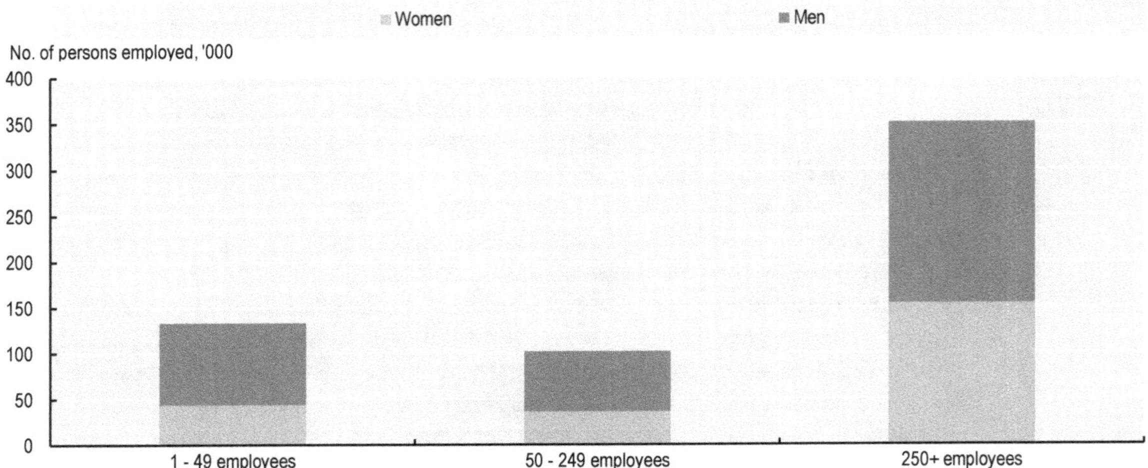

Source: Stats NZ, MFAT calculations (2021).

Conversely, there is a high representation of women in domestically focused services sectors. In low-export industries such as healthcare and education, women make up over 70% of the workforce, while other industries with limited exports such as public administration and retail and accommodation also have relatively high rates of employment of women. Construction is the only domestic-focused industry with a strong male employment bias.

The underrepresentation of women in high-export industries is an enduring feature that has changed little in recent years. For example, while the proportion of women's employment in manufacturing and mining has grown slightly since 2005 (up two and four percentage points respectively to 31% and 24%), employment of women in agriculture, forestry and fishing is unchanged (at 32%) and in transport, postal and warehousing has declined two percentage points (to 26%).

It is unclear whether there are specific barriers constraining women's participation in export industry occupations – such as skills/qualifications mismatches or biases against hiring women for these jobs – or whether it reflects different employment preferences of men and women.

Proportion of women working in export and tradable employment

Despite growth in the number of women in tradable employment, the proportion of women working in the export and tradable sectors as a share of total women's employment has actually fallen. This is due to the number of women in non-export-related jobs growing rapidly. Since 2005, women's employment in the tradable sector has grown by 91 000, including 46 000 more women in export-related jobs. However, this was more than offset by an increase of 259,000 in non-tradable employment (Figure 1.6). As a result, the proportion of women in export employment declined from 21.8% to 19.5% in 2021, and in tradable industries from 43.4% to 38.8% (Figure 1.7).

Figure 1.6. Women's export, tradable and non-tradable employment

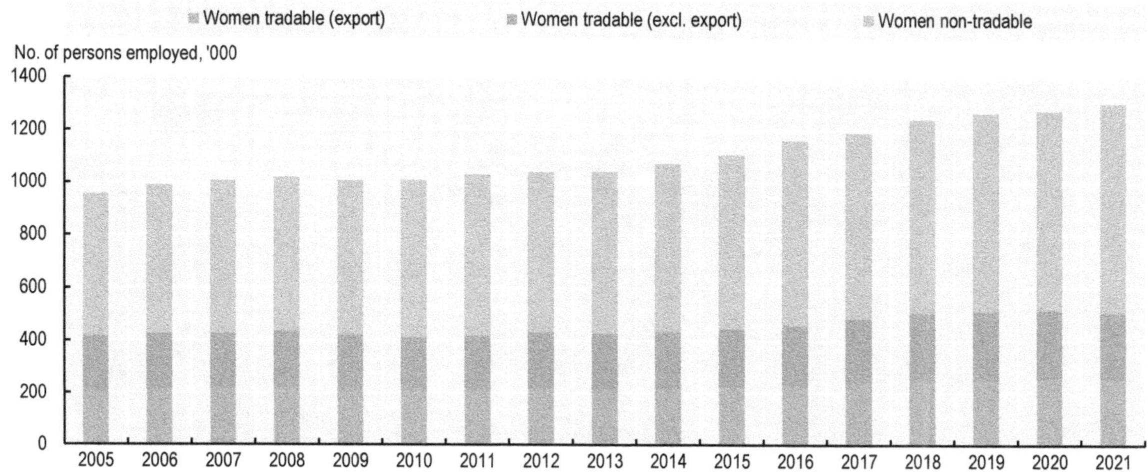

Note: Years to June quarter.
Source: Stats NZ, MFAT calculations (2021).

Figure 1.7. Employment in export and tradable sectors as share of total

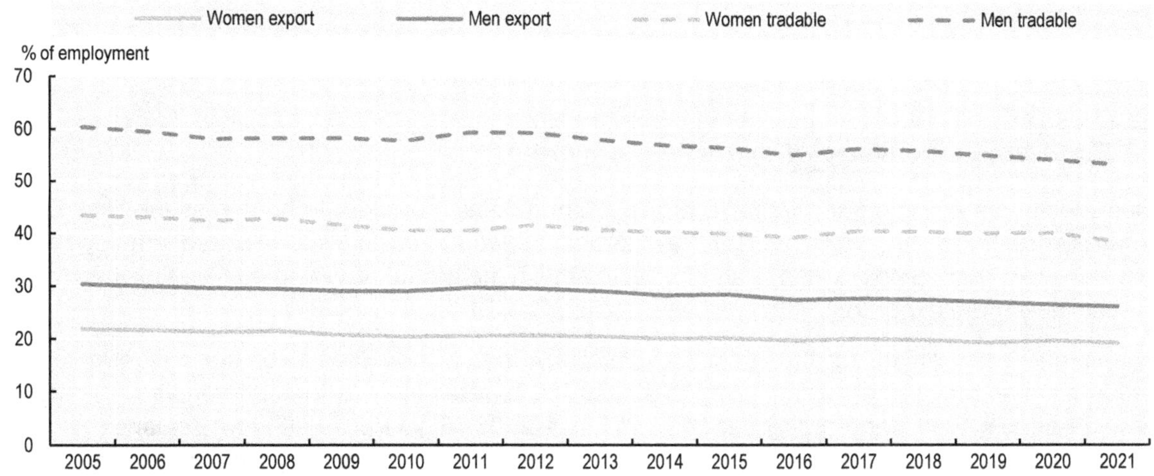

Note: Years to June quarter.
Source: Stats NZ, MFAT calculations (2021).

Proportion of women working in export employment by ethnicity

The top down methodology can be further extended to look at the intersection between gender and ethnicity.[4] Women, regardless of ethnicity, remain markedly less likely to be in export employment than men (Figure 1.8). Māori and Pasifika women are more likely to be in export employment than New Zealand European women. This in large part stems from relatively high employment of Māori women in export-oriented agriculture and related manufacturing sectors, while Pasifika women have relatively high employment in manufacturing and transport and warehousing. Similar industry composition figures drive the relatively higher proportion of Māori and Pasifika men in export employment.

Figure 1.8. Export employment by gender and ethnicity

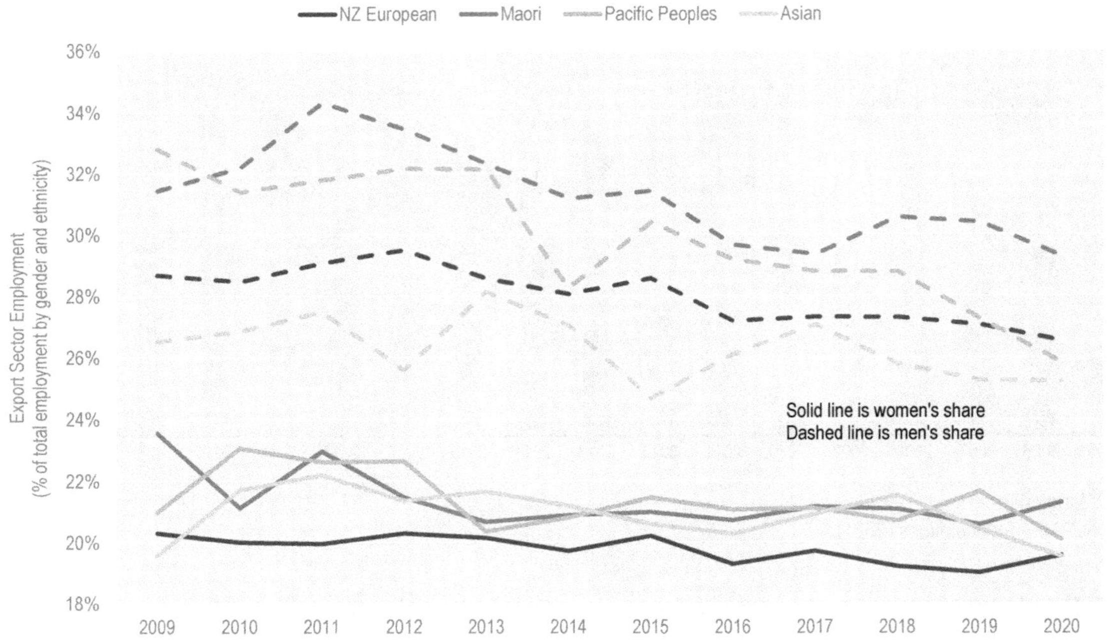

Note: Years to June quarter.
Source: Stats NZ, MFAT calculations (2021).

Economy-wide share of export employment

The declining share of export and tradable employment reflects a broader trend across the New Zealand economy. Since 2005, the proportion of New Zealand's workforce in export-related employment has steadily declined from 26.4% to 23.1% and tradable employment from 52.5% to 46.6%. This has matched similar declines in the export orientation of New Zealand's GDP.

This trend has been driven by the rapid growth of low-export industries over the past two decades. Industries such as government administration, construction, retail trade, and health and social care have led New Zealand's GDP and employment growth since 2005 (Figure 1.9). Of New Zealand's 15 fastest growing industries, only three have had a notable export focus: forestry and logging, mining, and support services for primary industries. Conversely, in agriculture – the industry with the highest export propensity – output in 2020 was broadly similar to 2005 levels in real terms, while real output in some sections of the manufacturing industry declined.

Employment growth has broadly followed these trends in output. Almost 80% of new employment since 2005 has been in services industries with low export propensities[5] (Figure 1.10). Meanwhile, in export-focused industries, there were 47 000 more people employed across the agriculture, forestry and fishing and transport, postal and warehousing industries in 2021 than in 2005. This was partially offset by 22 000 fewer jobs in manufacturing and negligible growth in mining employment, despite mining being the second-fastest growing export industry since 2005 in terms of output.

Figure 1.9. Real GDP growth since 2005 by industry and export ratios

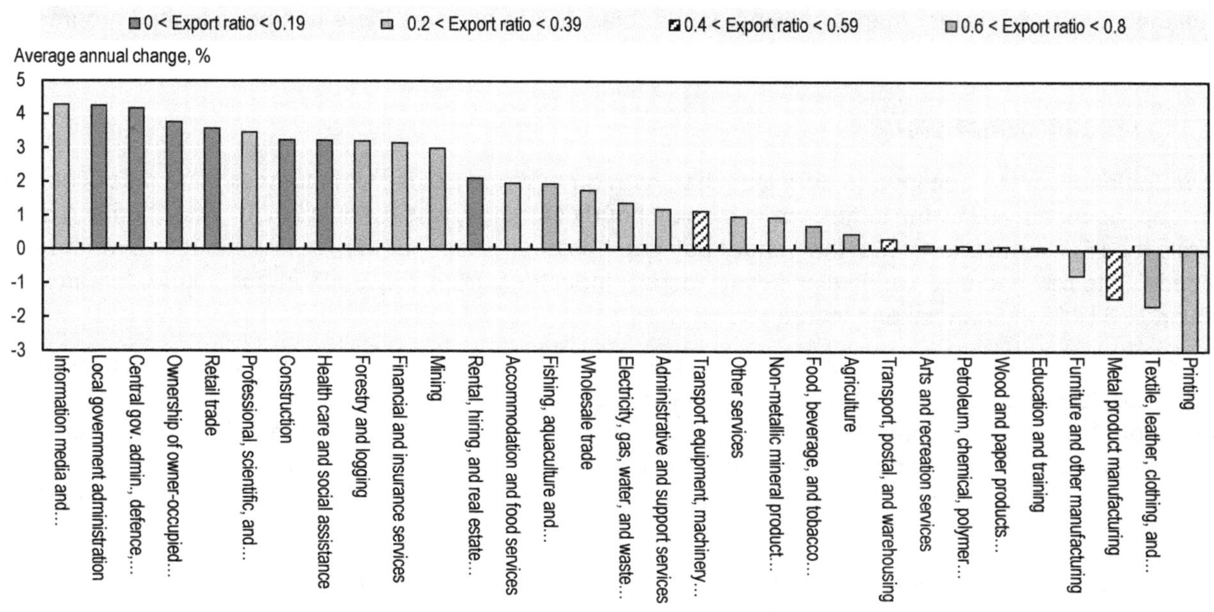

Source: Stats NZ, MFAT calculations (2021).

Figure 1.10. Employment growth since 2005 by broad industry

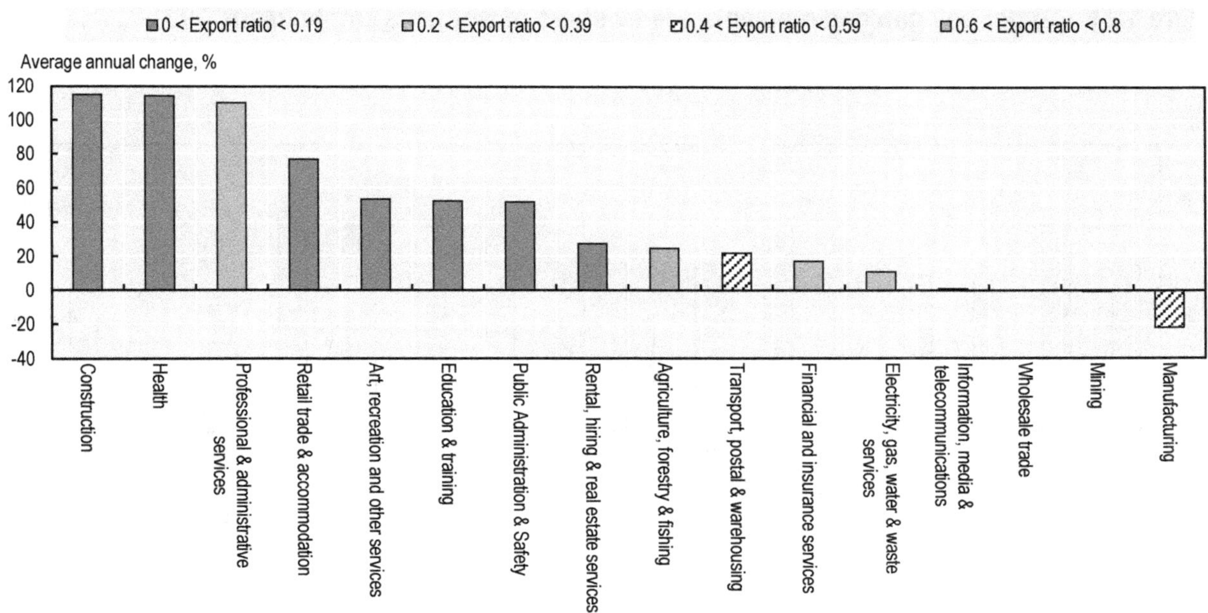

Source: Stats NZ, MFAT calculations (2021).

As a result, it appears from aggregate employment data that the declining share of women's export employment has been driven mainly by a structural decline in the share of export employment across New Zealand's economy, rather than a growing gender bias. It also appears there has been limited progress in increasing women's participation in export and trade-focused industries in recent years.

Gender wage gap

New Zealand women continue to earn less than men on average across all industries. The official gender pay gap, as measured by the difference in median hourly earnings, was 9.1% in 2021.[6] After trending down from over 15% in the late 1990s, the gender pay gap has been essentially flat at around 10% over the past decade. The pay gap also varies significantly across industries, from only 0.4% in agriculture, forestry and fishing to 31.0% in financial and insurance services.

While some studies have found that wages tend to be significantly lower in industries dominated by women, in New Zealand there appears little correlation at an aggregate level between the level of the median wage in an industry and the proportion of employment of women (Figure 1.11). For example, the median wage is higher in the health and education industries where women comprise over 70% of the workforce than in the male-dominated construction, transport, postal and warehousing, and agriculture, forestry and fishing industries.[7]

Similarly, gender wage gaps across industries do not appear to relate to the share of employment of women in those industries. For example, the gender wage gaps in the health and education industries where women are prevalent are 18.3% and 15.8% respectively; whereas in the construction, transport, postal and warehousing, and agriculture, forestry and fishing industries, where fewer women work, the gaps range from only 0.4% to 3.4%.

Figure 1.11. Gender pay gap and median wage by share of women's employment, 2021

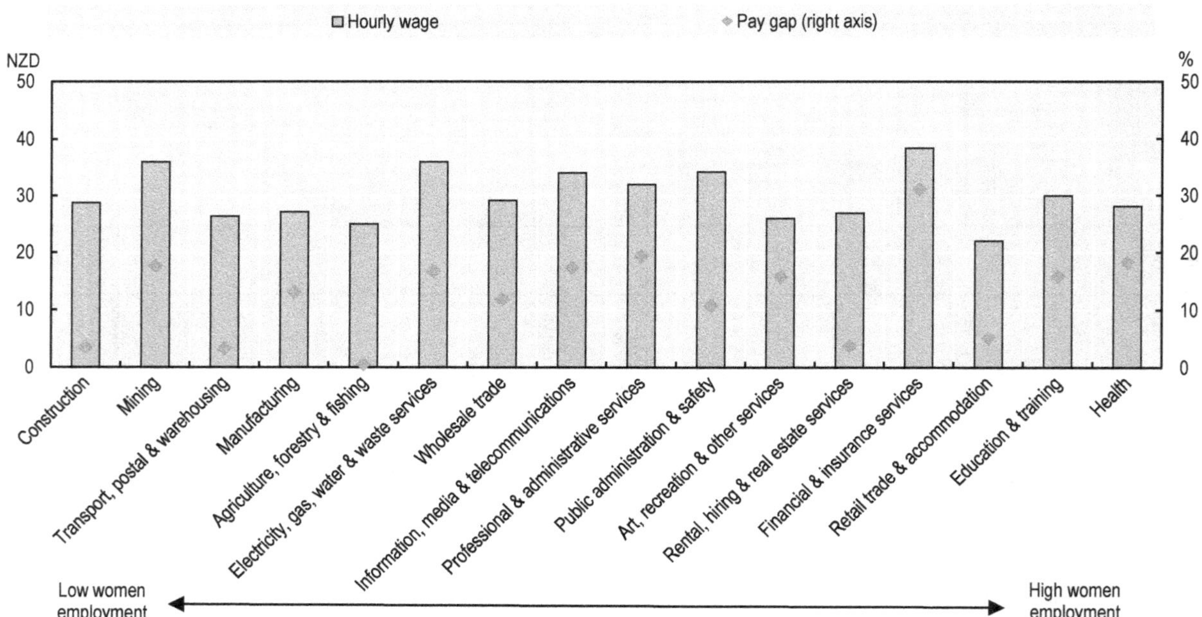

Source: Stats NZ, MFAT calculations (2021).

When considering gender wage gaps across occupation rather than industry, there is some evidence that gender pay disparities are larger in higher income occupations. The median hourly wage for women in high-earning professional roles is 15.0% less than for men, whereas for women in labourer, sales, or clerical and administration roles the gender wage gap ranges from 4.4% to 8.7%. A notable exception to this trend is in managerial roles, where the pay gap is 6.9%.

Other measures such as weekly and average earnings reveal wider pay gaps. For example, the gender pay gap as measured by average hourly wages was 10.6% in 2021, as the long upper tail for wages has a greater impact on the mean than the median and men are disproportionately represented in high-earning roles. Further, when measured as median weekly earnings, the gender pay gap was 23% in 2021. The firm-level analysis uses a similar median monthly earnings measure. The significant difference between hourly and weekly/monthly earnings reflects that women are almost twice as likely as men to work part-time and are less likely to work overtime, due to women shouldering more family responsibilities and unpaid work in the household.

Gender pay gap in export sectors

Estimates of the wage gaps between men and women in export and tradable employment also remain broadly similar to what they were a decade ago. They also remain consistently higher than the gender wage gap in non-tradable employment (Figure 1.12). The industry-weighted median wage for women in export employment in 2021 was 10.5% lower than for men, while in tradable employment it was 12.4% lower. This compares with an 8.9% wage gap in non-tradable employment.

Figure 1.12. Estimates of export, tradable and non-tradable gender wage gaps

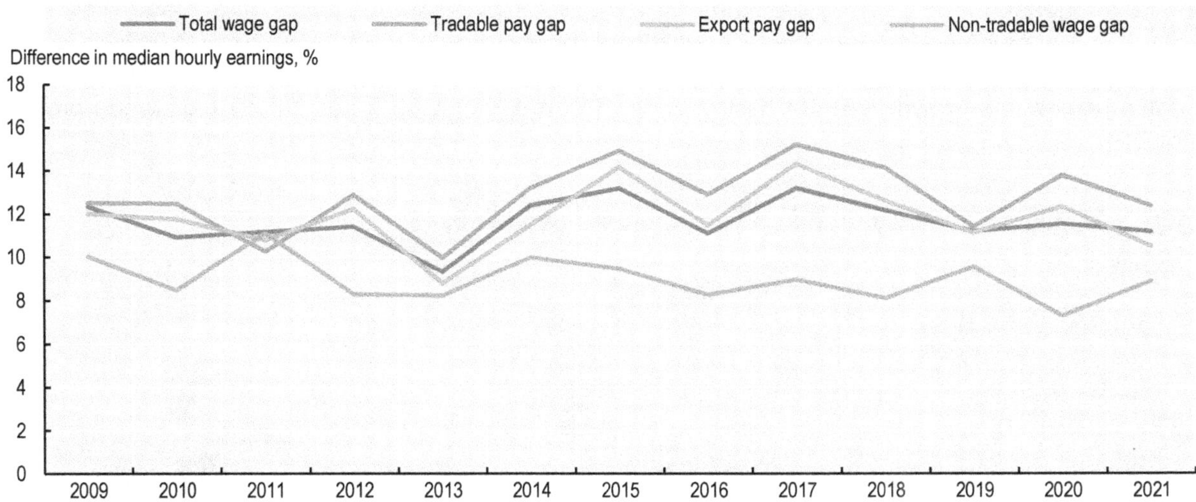

Note: These are industry-weighted estimates of the median wage gaps between males and females. For consistency, the 'Total wage gap' depicted here therefore differs from the official measure discussed elsewhere.
Source: Stats NZ, MFAT calculations (2021).

Larger gender pay gaps in export employment also emerge in the firm-level data using a median monthly earnings measure, with gender pay gaps of 23.6% for goods exporting firms and 21.6% for non-goods exporting firms. For direct goods exporters only the difference is even more marked at 26.4%. Furthermore, the differences appear larger for larger exporting firms, while interestingly the reverse is true of non-exporting firms (Figure 1.13).

Figure 1.13. Gender pay gap in average monthly earnings by firm size, 2018

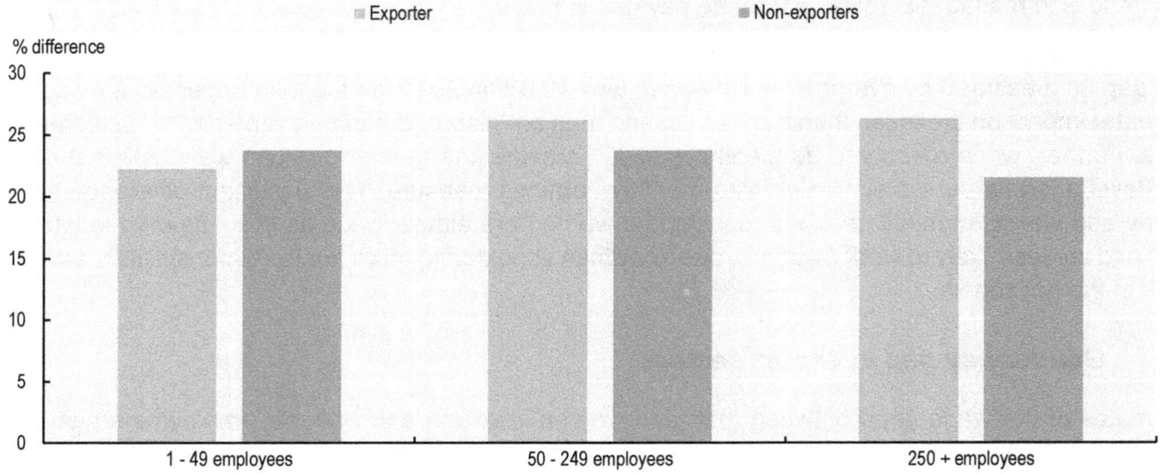

Source: Stats NZ, MFAT calculations (2021).

Women employees also appear to be benefiting less from participating in export activities than men when comparing export and non-export related wages for each gender, i.e. their "export pay premium". Men employed in goods exporting firms earn, on average, 11.2% more than men employed in non-exporting firms. By contrast, the export pay premium for women employees is only 8.1% on average. This higher export firm pay premium for men is replicated across most sectors (Figure 1.14). Similar findings emerge in the aggregate, top-down analysis. Furthermore, this gender difference between tradable and non-tradable wages has grown over the past decade, with men enjoying a particularly high wage premium since 2015.

Figure 1.14. Export firm pay premium by sector and gender, 2018

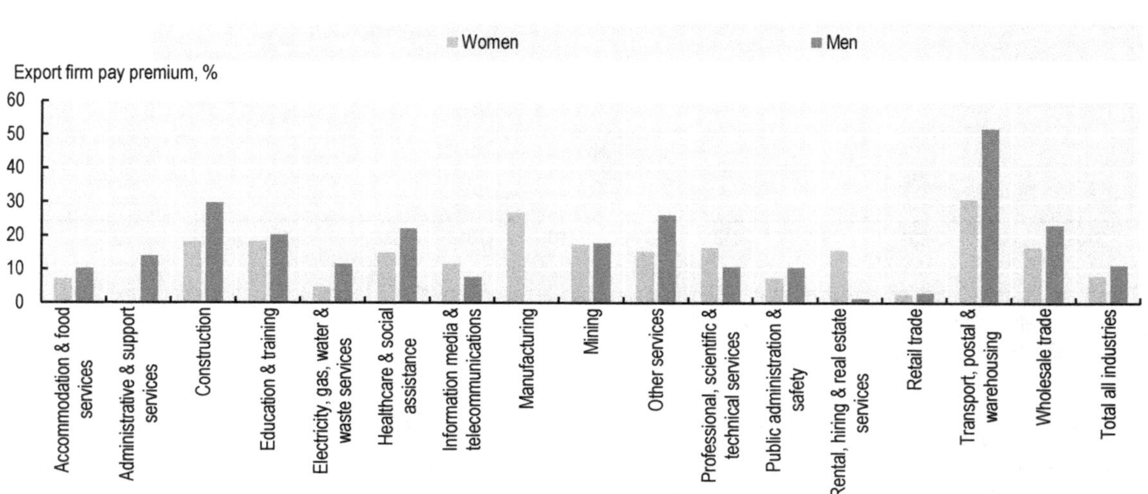

Note: Figure does not include pay premium data for the following sectors: Agriculture, fisheries and forestry (as all firms in this sector are considered exporters); Financial and insurance services (given that we would not expect these firms to export goods); Manufacturing, for male employees (due to Statistics NZ suppression requirements); and Arts and Recreation Services (the magnitude of the export pay premium is artificially high for this sector – due to the small number of exporting firms from this sector in our sample).
Source: Stats NZ, MFAT calculations (2021).

However, it is difficult from aggregate data to identify the drivers of the larger tradable gender disparities – in particular, to identify whether they relate to factors intrinsic to trade or other sources of gender discrimination. As seen in some other OECD countries, gender wage gaps in New Zealand tend to be larger in higher wage industries (Figure 1.15). Moreover, this trend is consistent across both higher exporting and lower exporting industries. It is also not clear that exporting industries have exceptionally large gender wage gaps across different levels of educational qualification. While industry pay disparities generally are larger and more varied for individuals with higher qualification levels, it is broadly consistent across exporting and domestically focused industries (Figure 1.16). In fact, women with bachelor's degrees or higher in the transport, postal and warehousing, and agriculture, forestry and fishing industries earn higher hourly median wages than men, although the sample sizes for these groups are relatively small.

Figure 1.15. Industry gender wage gaps and wage levels, 2021

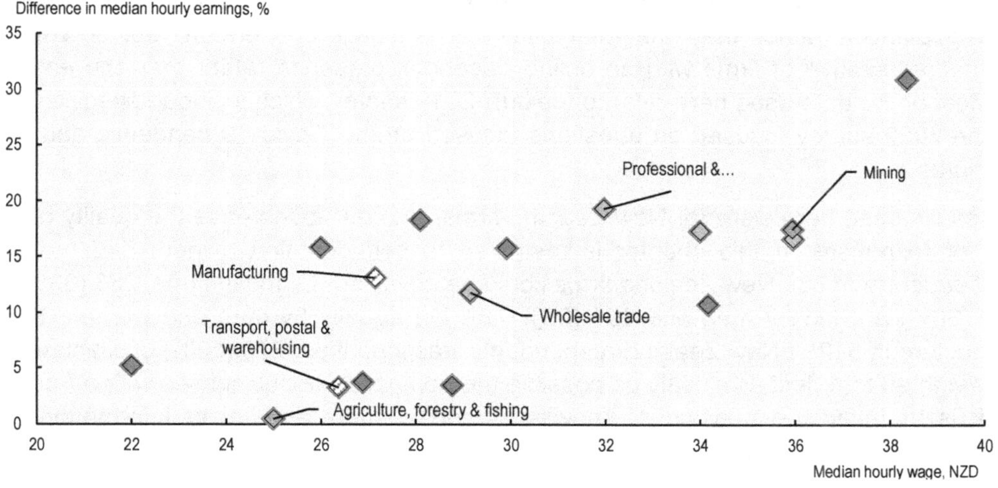

Source: Stats NZ, MFAT calculations (2021).

Figure 1.16. Industry gender wage gaps by educational qualification, 2021

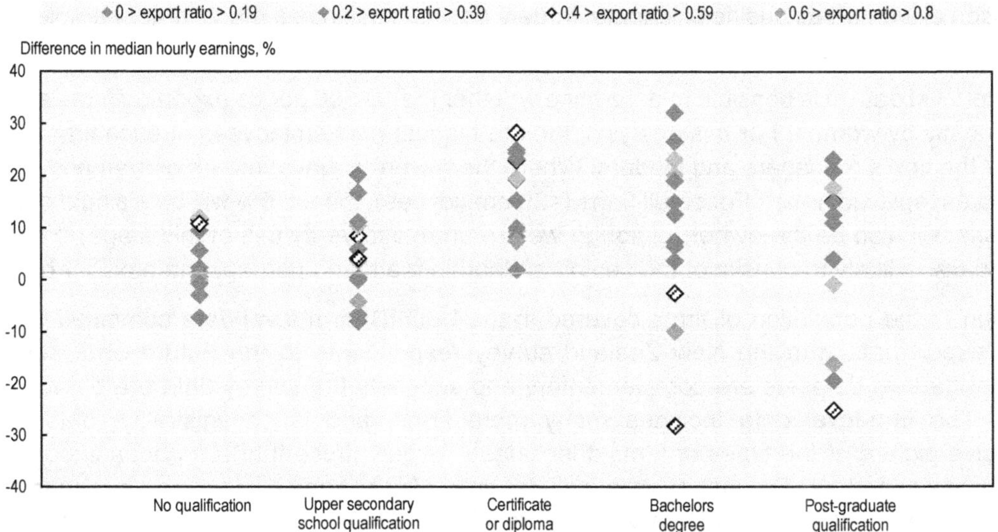

Note: Due to data unavailability, the Mining, Information, media & telecommunications, and Electricity, gas, water & waste services industries are not included
Source: Stats NZ, MFAT calculations (2021).

Women entrepreneurs, business owners and leaders

Methodology and data

This section focusses on women's participation in trade as business owners and leaders, with a focus on better understanding the characteristics of their businesses and the challenges they face to trading. An overview of the business characteristics of women-owned and women-led businesses, their situation *vis-à-vis* trade, and the challenges they face will make use of the *OECD-World Bank-Facebook Future of Business* survey of firms with an online presence on Facebook. The bi-annual survey includes questions about perceptions of current and future economic activity, including trade, as well challenges and business characteristics, including the gender of the owner/manager. The survey aims to give a snapshot of businesses, mostly small and medium-sized, with an online presence. Over 700 000 Facebook page owners have taken the survey, out of an estimated population of 80 million businesses that have created a Facebook business page.[8] The survey was weighted in accordance with the Facebook page administrator population rather than the total business population. Therefore the survey should be regarded as representative of firms with an online Facebook presence rather than the entire business population. Most of the data used here refer to the July 2019 survey which included specific trade-related questions. The 2020 survey focused on questions focused on the Covid-19 pandemic and government support measures.

The survey results used here were for New Zealand firms. In order to increase the quality of responses, the analysis of responses in this chapter is restricted to self-identified owners and managers. The management structure of 868 New Zealand firms could be identified. Of those firms, 283 (33%) are led by women, 331 (38%) are led by men and 254 (29%) are led equally by men and women. Similarly, the ownership structure in 512 of New Zealand respondents was identified, 273 (53%) of which were women. Results are weighted to reflect as closely as possible the population of businesses with a Facebook page as Facebook is "in a unique position of knowing a considerable amount of information about both respondents and non-respondents" (Schneider, 2020[2]).

It will be seen that the vast majority of the firms surveyed in this way are in services sectors. This analysis complements the analysis focussing on New Zealand women's participation in goods exporting as entrepreneurs, business owners and leaders. That analysis primarily utilises the firm-level data set described at the beginning of the "Women workers" section. The analysis mostly focuses on the slightly wider definition of women as business leaders, largely because this has a much larger sample size to work with in the firm-level dataset.

From the firm-level data, it is possible to determine whether the 10 500 goods exporting firms are led mostly by men or mostly by women. For this analysis, the 5% highest paid employees in each firm are assumed to constitute the firm's managers and leaders. Where there were equal numbers of men and women, they are regarded as "split led firms". For small firms (<20 employees), the top 5% will be a single person, which in many cases will also be the owner (although we are unable to verify this at this stage). For the largest firms, the top 5% is likely to consist of the senior leadership team and perhaps the next tier of managers.

A comparison of the population of firms covered in the LBD-IDI firm level data combined with customs import and export data with the New Zealand survey respondents to the Future of Business Survey suggests that the two datasets are complementary and suggests the survey data are broadly significant (Table 1.1). The firm-level data includes many more firms, and is administrative data so gives a comprehensive picture of the types of firms it includes – largely those that are goods exporters or firms that sell to goods exporters. The survey data includes many fewer firms – it includes less than 1 000 firms whereas the comprehensive LBD-IDI dataset covers 160 000 firms. FOBS includes more services firms, but covers agriculture and construction firms less well than the administrative data. Its bias is toward those firms that are digitally active, since the survey is online. It surveys many fewer firms than are included in the administrative data but includes services firms that do not export indirectly through goods exporting firms, and includes some additional qualitative information such as the challenges faced by entrepreneurs. Interestingly, the FOBS includes a slightly smaller share of micro-firms and a slightly larger representation of medium-sized and larger firms, than the administrative dataset. Both datasets suggest that around 15% of New Zealand firms export.

The quantitative analysis was complemented by a qualitative process of engaging women entrepreneurs and business leaders. The qualitative analysis consisted of structured discussions with New Zealand women entrepreneurs focused on the challenges they face growing their businesses internationally, the discrimination they have faced as business leaders, and the support they have received. These discussions were facilitated by New Zealand's trade promotion agency, New Zealand Trade and Enterprise (NZTE).

Table 1.1. Firm coverage in the LPD-IDI administrative data and the Future of Business Survey

Number of firms and share in the total number of firms covered in each dataset

	Firm-level data (1)				Future of Business Survey			
	Goods exporter (direct or indirect)	Share	Non-exporter	Share (%)	Exporter	Share (%)	Non-exporter	Share (%)
Agriculture, Forestry and Fishing	21264	13.37	0 (2)	0.00	17	2.79	27	4.56
Construction	81	0.05	22,620	14.22	4	0.65	41	6.86
Manufacturing	1419	0.89	9,117	5.73	16	2.67	26	4.28
Services	2253	1.42	102,315	64.32	49	8.22	417	69.97
Total	25017	15.73	134,052	84.27	85	14.33	511	85.67

Note: 1. Combining New Zealand's administrative data sets, the Longitudinal Business Database (LBD) and the Integrated Data Infrastructure (IDI). All agricultural firms were assumed to be exporters.

Business characteristics[9]

One factor in the success and survival of a firm is the motivation for starting the business. Most entrepreneurs in New Zealand start their businesses by choice. The main reason for both women and men to found their own business is to achieve a better work life balance: this reason is given by about 50% of both women and men. Other main reasons for going into entrepreneurship are to pursue a passion or interest, greater independence, and to make more money. A minority of entrepreneurs (about 14% of both women and men) are *opportunity entrepreneurs*, i.e. they have gone into business to commercialise a specific product or develop an idea (Box 1.1). Slightly fewer women entrepreneurs (9%) than men (10%) in New Zealand are *necessity entrepreneurs,* i.e. they have founded or joined their businesses because they have no other employment opportunities. Contrary to the situation in OECD countries more generally, more New Zealand women (11%) have taken over family businesses than men (8%). A substantial share of both women and men business owners – close to 30% – are *sidepreneurs*, i.e. they also have another activity, usually paid employment in another firm.

New Zealand businesses owned by women tend to be younger than those owned by men. Over one-third of business led by men have been in operation for ten years or longer whereas less than one in five of businesses led by women have been operating for ten years or more.

Box 1.1. Types of entrepreneurship

Entrepreneurs found their businesses for a complex set of reasons, and many of them depend on the other economic opportunities available to them. Necessity entrepreneurs are unemployed or cannot find quality employment. Their only viable employment option is to found a business. In times of high economic growth, necessity entrepreneurship declines. Flexibility entrepreneurs found their businesses because workforce policies do not accommodate their caregiving responsibilities or they desire more control over when and where they work. While some necessity and flexibility entrepreneurs grow successful businesses, for the most part they return to the labour force when they can. Opportunity entrepreneurs see possibilities in the market that they want to exploit. They are more likely to enter the market in good economic times than in bad. These businesses tend to have a higher rate of survival and better growth prospects. Part-time entrepreneurship is often called sidepreneurship. The rate of growth in the number of sidepreneurs is often greater than for all ventures

Source: American Express (2019[3]).

The vast majority of women-owned and women-led businesses are in services sectors (Figure 1.17). Close to 90% of women-led firms with a Facebook business page are in services, compared with 54% of men-led firms. Men-led firms far outnumber women-led firms in construction and agriculture, and are more prevalent in the manufacturing sector.

Services subsectors where most women own and lead businesses are personal services,[10] hospitality, education services, retail and wholesale trade, and professional and scientific services.[11] Men tend to own and lead businesses in professional and scientific services and retail and wholesale trade, followed by the media, information and communications sector,[12] and the hospitality sector.

Figure 1.17. The vast majority of women-owned and women-led firms are in services

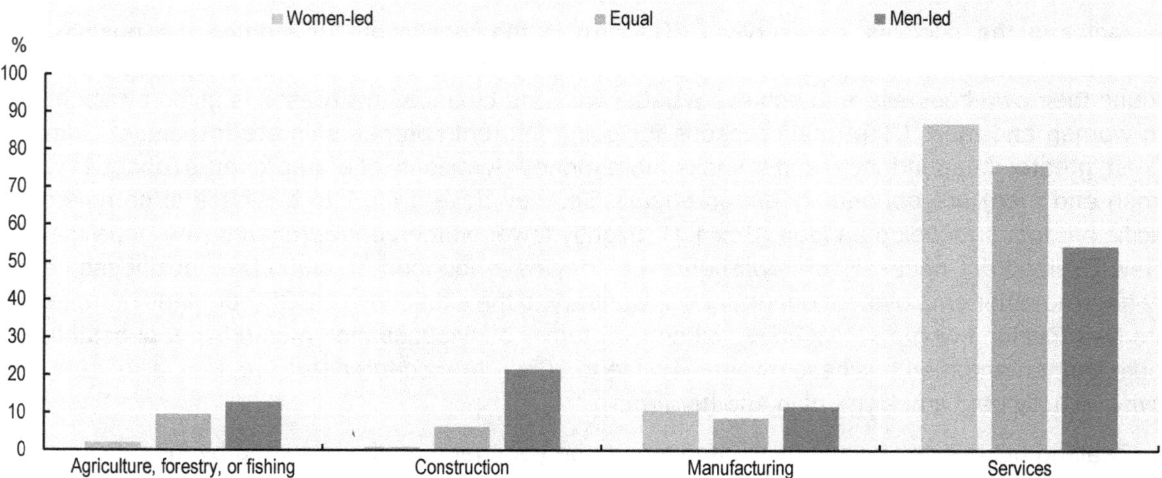

Note: Firms based in New Zealand with a Facebook presence.
Source: Facebook-OECD-World Bank Future of Business survey, June 2019.

As in other OECD countries, women-owned and women-led businesses are smaller than those owned and led by men. Women entrepreneurs in New Zealand are much less likely than men to have employees (Figure 1.18). They are more likely than men to lead micro- or small enterprises (less than 20 employees). In larger businesses, the gulf between women and men in ownership and management is substantial. It is particularly wide in medium-sized (50-250 employees) and large firms (more than 250 employees) which represent 16% and 14% of men-led firms respectively, compared with 7% and 6% of women-led firms.

Even in services sub-sectors where women dominate, their businesses are smaller. In personal services, retail trade, hospitality, healthcare and professional services, women-owned and women-led businesses tend to be smaller than those owned and led by men.

Figure 1.18. Women led firms are smaller than those led by men

Share of New Zealand firms by number of employees

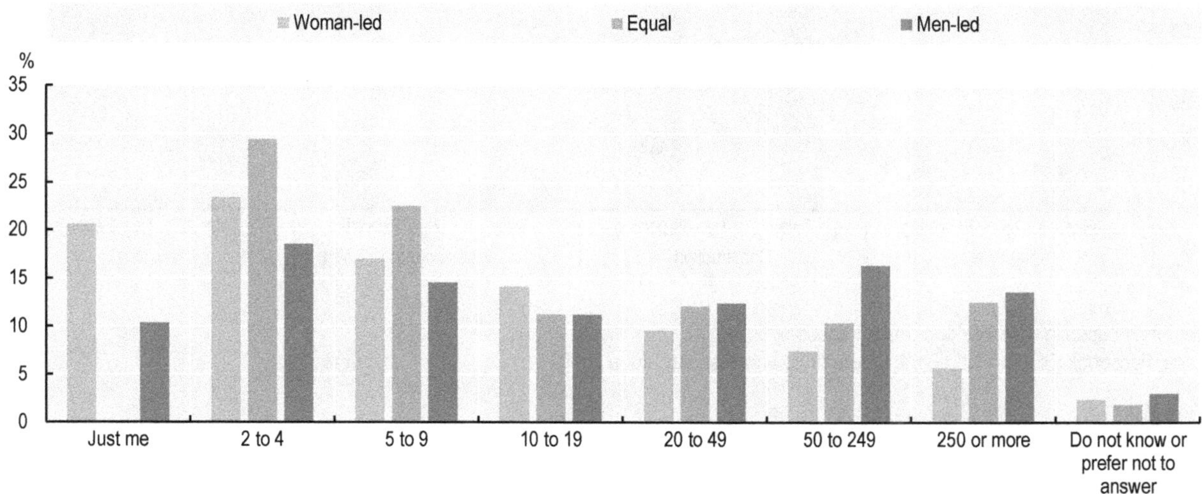

Note: Firms based in New Zealand with a Facebook presence.
Source: Facebook-OECD-World Bank Future of Business survey, June 2019.

Women entrepreneurs in trade[13]

Overall, as in many other OECD countries, women entrepreneurs in New Zealand trade less than their male counterparts (Figure 1.19) This finding is driven mostly by smaller enterprises. Since smaller enterprises tend to trade less, and women-led businesses tend to be smaller, they trade less overall than men-led businesses. However, although the vast majority of micro and small firms do not trade, women-led sole proprietor firms (with no employees) in New Zealand actually trade more than men-led firms of the same size. Women-led medium- and large-sized enterprises tend to trade less than their men-led equivalents. However, women-led firms that trade tend to export to more countries than their male counterparts, regardless of firm size. Moreover, there is a small subset of women business leaders of medium and large enterprises who export very extensively – to more than 11 countries – and on average they export to more countries than their male counterparts. In services sectors, women-led firms trade almost as much as men-led ones which is notable given that some services where women work (personal services, childcare, etc.) are less traded across borders.

As is the case in many OECD countries, women-owned and women-led businesses tend to export more to individual consumers and export less to other businesses, than men-led firms. This indicates that in order to expand exports, they will need to increase their extensive margins, i.e. increase the number of customers, rather than the intensive margin, i.e. the size of each order.

Figure 1.19. Women-led firms trade less than men-led firms

Share of New Zealand firms and share of firms that export by gender

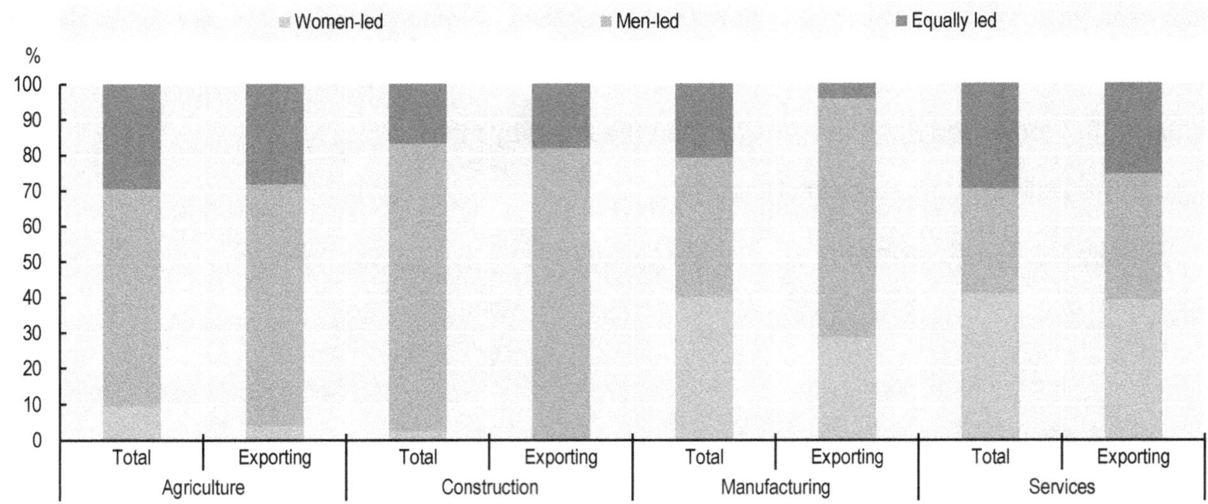

Note: Firms based in New Zealand with a Facebook presence.
Source: Facebook-OECD-World Bank Future of Business survey, June 2019.

Women-owned and women-led businesses engage with their clients online

The Covid-19 pandemic has shown the potential and importance of e-commerce. Even before the pandemic, women-owned and women-led businesses in OECD countries, and even more so in New Zealand, engaged online more extensively than their male counterparts. Women-owned and women-led businesses are more likely than those owned and led by men to receive more than half of their orders online. They are substantially less likely than their male counterparts to receive less than a quarter of their business from online sales.

Challenges to business expansion and trade

When asked specifically about challenges to trade, both women and men business leaders indicate the biggest challenge is 'distance to foreign markets'. Perhaps unsurprisingly this challenge was cited more often in New Zealand than in any other OECD country. Moreover, this challenge is cited equally by leaders of small and larger firms. Although there is no way that trade policies can bring markets closer, distance can become somewhat less challenging to exporters in situations of high levels of air transport connectivity and digital services and connectivity (for more information on this, see section on New Zealand's regulatory environment for services trade and Benz and Jaax (2022, forthcoming[4]). It should be noted that 'poor internet connection to sell online' was not a concern for any of the New Zealand business leaders in the Facebook survey.

The second largest challenge to exporting expressed by women business leaders is navigating foreign regulations. Navigating customs regulations was cited among the top five challenges by both women and men exporters and was cited as a common concern both by leaders of small and larger firms.[14] Just over one-fifth of women business owners who expressed difficulties exporting indicated that compliance with customs regulations was a major challenge for their business. There may be a role for export promotion services in main export markets in informing New Zealand women exporters of regulations abroad, and aiding them to manage those constraints.

About one-fifth of women business owners that expressed difficulties exporting indicated that e-payment systems represent a challenge, and women seem to indicate this more frequently than men. The sectors most impacted by poor online payment alternatives are the retail trade and textiles and clothing sectors. This could also be an area of exploration for New Zealand's export promotion experts, either in terms of information or technical assistance in navigating existing e-payment solutions, or tailoring needs to different export markets.

Interestingly, few women entrepreneurs indicate that they experience challenges finding overseas partners, which is one of the main challenges experienced by men entrepreneurs. This may be due to women exporting more to individuals, preferring to sell their products and services through distributors or online platforms, or to the smaller size of their businesses.

Contrary to many OECD countries, women business leaders surveyed through Facebook in New Zealand overall do not rank financing as one of the main challenges to business expansion. This finding may be driven by smaller firms; in medium-sized enterprises, financing is a more frequently cited challenge. This may point to the small amount of capital that women usually have to start their businesses. In OECD countries in general, women request less credit, and obtain less than they request, and so start their businesses with less capital. As businesses grow, access to capital becomes more of an issue and is a problem more often cited by women leaders of firms with 20 or more employees than by men. Similarly, few women cited 'export financing' among their main challenges, which may reflect the nature of the services they are selling, much of it online, and therefore with more limited capital needs. In fact, only among entrepreneurs in the textiles and clothing sector was obtaining export financing considered a challenge.

Impact of the COVID-19 pandemic on women and men entrepreneurs[15]

The year 2020 represented a challenging environment for entrepreneurs, both women and men. The restrictions of movement due to the pandemic, coupled with drops in demand for many goods and services and disruptions to supply chains, meant that many small businesses were strongly impacted. Despite these challenges, women-owned businesses in New Zealand have shown great resilience. Fewer women business owners declared that their levels of activity in 2020 were lower than before the pandemic, compared with men business owners (Figure 1.20). Moreover, slightly more women owners indicated that their activity was the same or higher than before the pandemic, as compared with men.[16]

The results regarding impacts of the pandemic will need to be confirmed with the 2021 survey data. This is particularly true as New Zealand's most restrictive measures came somewhat later in the pandemic compared to many other OECD countries. One positive aspect that may explain women entrepreneurs' resilience during 2020 is their large online presence that may have allowed them to navigate the changes in delivery of goods and services.[17] Globally, businesses that reported higher shares of digital sales were also more likely to have reported more robust sales during the pandemic period (Facebook, 2021[5]).

Figure 1.20. Women-owned firms are highly resilient

Stated level of businesses' activity in 2020 compared to 2019 by gender of their owner

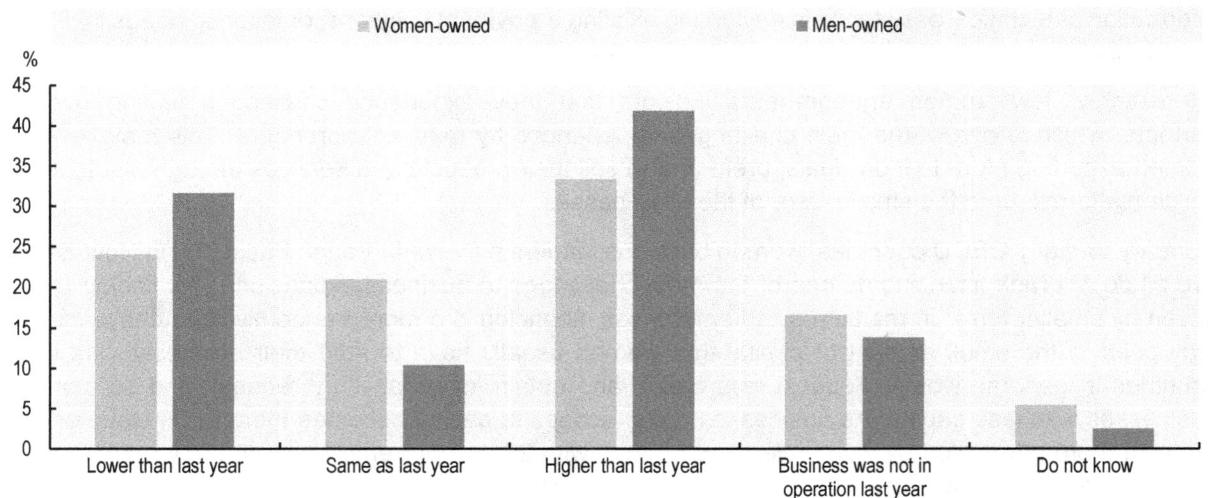

Note: Firms based in New Zealand with a Facebook presence.
Source: Facebook-OECD-World Bank Future of Business survey, 2020. Monthly surveys were conducted from the end of May until the end of October 2020, with an additional wave fielded at the end of December 2020.

Some survey responses related to the state of businesses during the pandemic suggests some of the underlying challenges faced by women entrepreneurs. A larger percentage of women business owners (5.4%) than men (2.5%) did not report knowing whether their business is doing better or worse than in the previous year. More women than men also indicated they had founded their business in the last year, which mirrors the finding that women-owned and women-led businesses are younger and that a minority of entrepreneurs are *opportunity entrepreneurs,* i.e. they form their businesses to pursue a market opportunity or innovation, a category of businesses that tends to open when economies are performing well.

Women as leaders of goods exporting firms[18]

Using New Zealand's firm-level data for goods exporters, 82% of goods exporting firms are majority-men led, compared with 15% that are majority women-led. By comparison, firms producing goods led by men made up 69% of non-exporting firms and 28% were led by women. Exporting firms led by men accounted for over 96% of exports sold by these firms, with women-led firms accounting for just 3% of export values (Figure 1.21).[19] This is stark evidence of unequal participation at the senior leadership level across firms in general and exporting firms in particular. It is also a likely contributor to the gender pay gaps examined in earlier sections.

Women-led firms have a marginally higher export propensity than men- or split-owned firms. So while women appear to be significantly less likely to lead a firm (including an export firm), those firms they do lead are marginally more willing to sell overseas (31%) than men- or split-owned firms (25% and 19%, respectively). A key factor behind this is the higher export propensity of small (<50 employees) businesses led by women. For medium and large firms the differences in export propensity between women and men led firms are small.

Figure 1.21. Exporting firms by gender of firm leadership, 2021

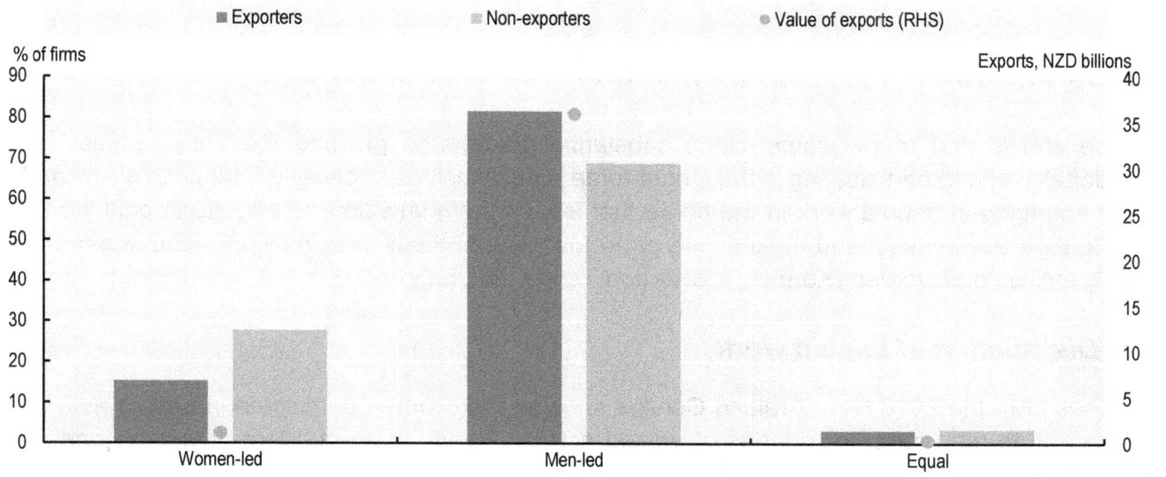

Source: Stats NZ, MFAT calculations (2021).

Figure 1.22. Export propensity by gender of leader and firm size, 2021

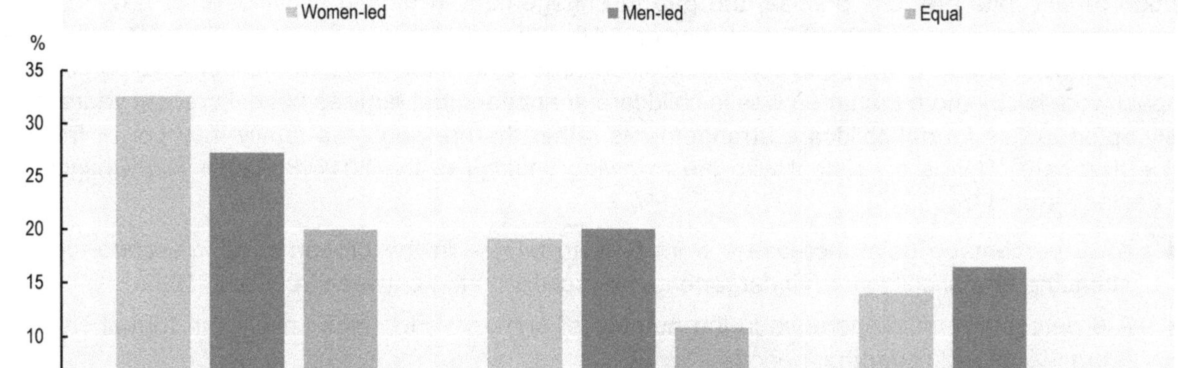

Source: Stats NZ, MFAT calculations (2021).

Women as owners of goods exporting firms

While firm-level data on ownership is limited, it is possible to investigate export characteristics of firms denoted as working proprietors in New Zealand's administrative data. Working proprietors accounted for NZD 14.8 billion of goods exports in 2018 and 7 000 exporting firms. Two-thirds of exporting working proprietors were men, while 14% were women and 20% were jointly owned. The high share of the latter reflects the inclusion of "indirect exporters" from the agricultural sector, of which a large number are family-run farms and orchards.

The insights from this subset of working proprietors largely mirror those of the leadership analysis. Men working proprietor exporters are currently more productive and pay higher average salaries than women working proprietors, though the differences are less stark than for firms led by men or women. Similar to the analysis of business leaders, women working proprietors have a marginally higher propensity to export. This result is driven by the higher export propensity of small women-owned businesses.

Barriers to women's participation in trade and labour markets

Evidence shows that many women face substantial barriers to growing their businesses, including internationally, and to participating in the labour force. These include accessing finance to a similar degree to men, engaging in unpaid work in the home that leaves them less time to engage in paid work and to devote to their businesses, and making use of professional and business networks that seem to be less than fully inclusive of women (Korinek, Moïsé and Tange, 2021[6]).

Distribution of unpaid work

Responses from the 2018 New Zealand Census showed that women participate in unpaid activities at a higher rate than men for all categories of unpaid activity. Nearly three-quarters of women participate in household work, while only two-thirds of men undertake similar activities. Similarly, 27% of women were engaged in childcare in 2018 compared to 21% of men, and nearly twice as many women were involved in caring for an ill or disabled family member as men. This mirrors findings from the Stats NZ 2009 time use survey, which found that, on average, women engage in nearly twice the amount of unpaid work as men (4.4 hours per day for women versus 2.4 per day for men).

Although recent data are less precise, the gap in engagement in unpaid activities may have reduced somewhat in recent years. The 2018 Census indicated that the proportion of the population that participates in all categories of unpaid activity has decreased since 2006. One of the areas where women's participation in unpaid work fell by more than men was in childcare. It appears that families have, in recent years, more readily opted to use formal childcare arrangements rather than relying on a family member or friend to provide that care. This is consistent with the following findings of the 2017 Statistics NZ "Childcare in New Zealand survey":

- A 10 percentage point increase – from 54% to 64% – in the proportion of preschool children attending formal childcare (kindergartens, playschools, etc.) between 2009 and 2017.
- A 6 percentage point increase in the number of primary school-age children in formal childcare (from 9% to 15%) over that period.

A more recent survey indicated that lockdowns during the COVID-19 pandemic had an equalising effect on the participation of New Zealand men and women in unpaid activities (Westpac New Zealand, Deloitte, 2021[7]). The survey found that during New Zealand's pre-Delta lockdowns, women did 5% more paid work than in a typical week, and 7% less housework and had 6% less care responsibilities. Conversely, men did 4% more housework and 4% more care responsibilities, with no change to their paid work.

This sits in contrast to the experience in much of the rest of the world, where the COVID-19 pandemic, and associated lockdowns, appear to have had a disproportionately negative effect on women's participation in paid work (McKinsey Global Institute, 2020[8]). This is perhaps because of New Zealand's relatively short lockdowns relative to other economies. It remains to be seen whether changing attitudes towards working-from-home precipitated by these lockdowns will mean that these positive changes become permanent.

Figure 1.23. Percentage of 2018 NZ Census respondents participating in selected unpaid activities and change in participation rate since 2006

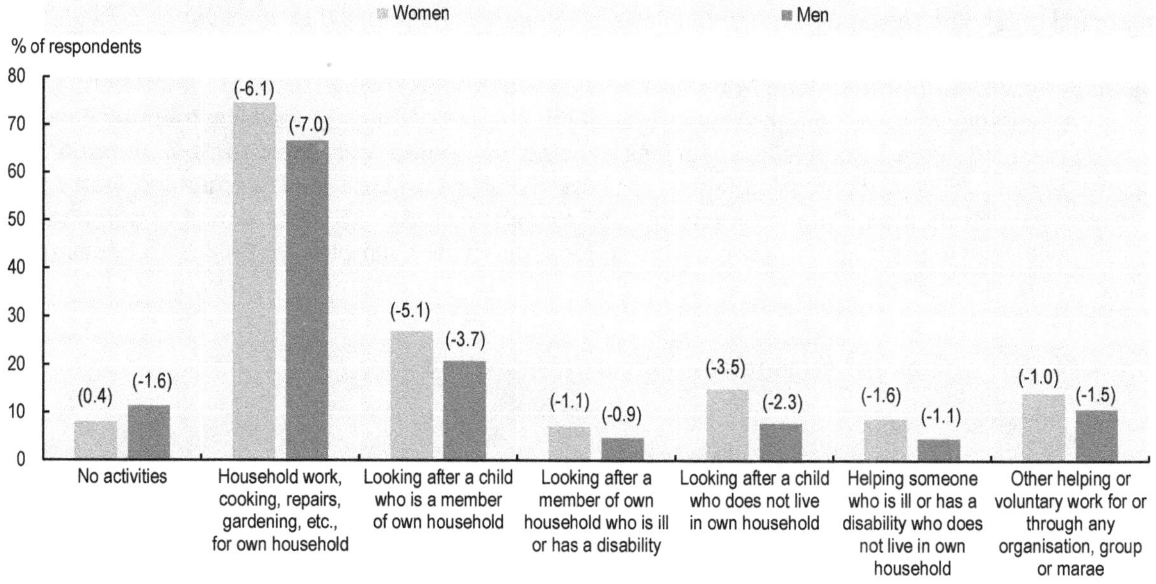

Source: Stats NZ, MFAT calculations (2021).

Access to finance

The Future of Business survey data suggested that access to finance was less of a challenge for women-led exporters in New Zealand than elsewhere in OECD countries. However, this challenge was raised by women exporters and business leaders during the consultative process. Problems accessing finance seem to be even more acute for Māori women business owners and leaders (BERL, 2022[9]). It is possible to link firm responses to the New Zealand Business Operations Survey (BOS), which asks questions about access to debt and equity finance, to their administrative data in the LBD. Because the BOS is a survey rather than administrative data, the number of firms for which leadership by gender can be determined falls to around 5 300, of which 1 365 are exporters. Just over 100 of those export firms were women-led. Whilst the number of firms is relatively small, the way the BOS sample is constructed, with a skew to larger firms, means export coverage is relatively high (NZD 32 billion, 58% of goods exports).

Within this relatively narrow sample, 8% of women-led goods exporting firms had sought access to equity finance, and 24% to debt finance, within the latest financial year. In both cases, this was lower than for men-led firms at 10% and 35% respectively. The rates were similar for non-goods exporting firms, with again women-led firms much less likely to have sought finance. For both women- and men-led firms, the reason finance was not sought was usually because it was not needed (about 75% for equity finance and about 85-90% for debt finance). A possible contributing factor to lower rates of women-led firms seeking financing is advice. About 20% of women-led export firms sought advice on debt or equity finance, while about 30% of men-led firms did so.

Equity raised by women-led and men-led firms in New Zealand

From a sample of firms that raised investor equity,[20] on average over the last ten years 11% of those firms were led by women, compared with 85% of equity-raising firms that were led by men, and 4% of firms were led by both women and men (Figure 1.24). The sector of activity where most firms raised capital was the information technology sector, with 48 men-led firms and four firms led by women receiving funding in New

Zealand since 2011. Other leading sectors of activity where men-led firms raised equity were the media (17 firms) and financial sectors (16 firms). Women-led firms raised equity in financial sector (four firms) and the wellness sector (three firms).

The amount of funding raised by women-led firms compared with those led by men varies considerably by year, but is always substantially less per firm. Over the last ten years, men-led firms received 97% of the total equity raised, with women-led firms raising only 3% of equity in New Zealand. In the period of 2015 to 2019, on average, women-led firms raised 17% of the amount of funding raised by men-led firms, which means women-led firms raised six times less funding compared with their male counterparts. This compares unfavourably to women-led firms in mainland Europe: in Germany, women-led start-ups raise three times less funds than male-led start-ups; in France they raise 2.5 times less; but compares more favourably with the United Kingdom, where women-led firms raise 13 times less (Boston Consulting Group, 2019[10]).

Figure 1.24. Few women-led firms raise equity in New Zealand

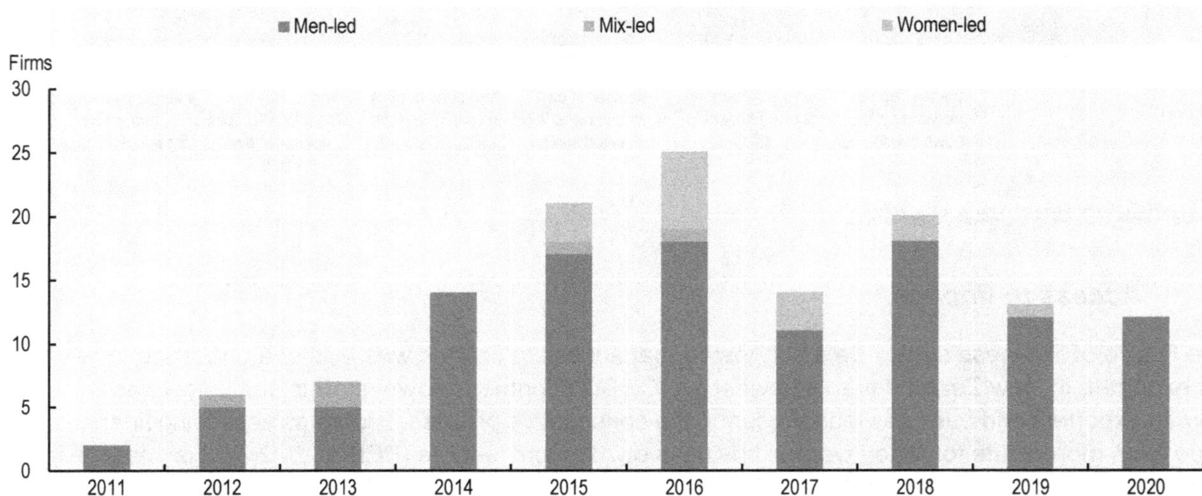

Source: Crunchbase and Dealroom databases.

Women consumers

Unlike women's economic roles as workers and business leaders, in their role as consumers trade impacts cannot be measured directly. Consumption patterns are generally collected at the household level, with no breakdown within households by gender. Instead of measuring the impacts of trade and trade policies on women directly, it is possible to measure price changes due to trade and trade policies and their effects on different types of households, such as couples, single dwellers, two-parent families and single-parent families, and on households at different income levels. Although this analysis does not apply specifically to women within households, they are disproportionately represented in certain household categories, such as single-parent households and elderly single dwellers. This analysis may be considered to go beyond the scope of the impact of trade on women and encompass more vulnerable populations.

The distributional implications of trade impacts on consumer prices

Following the framework described in Luu et al (2020[11]) the OECD's CGE model METRO (OECD, 2020[12]) is used to examine the extent to which different households are exposed to trade-driven changes in consumer prices resulting from trade policy changes.[21] A stylised hypothetical tariff simulation is conducted where New Zealand increases its tariffs to 25% on all imports from all trade partners[22] excluding Australia, which produces changes in consumer prices on the 65 commodities in the model. The results on commodity price changes are then linked to information from New Zealand's 2019 Household Economic Survey[23] describing expenditure patterns of different socio economic groups. Linking the model results and the household survey allows for comparing the exposure, measured by changes in purchasing power, across different household characteristics – for this analysis, household structure.

A household's exposure to trade-driven policy changes will depend on the price changes of the commodities they consume and the extent to which the household consumes that commodity. If price changes are concentrated in the goods and services consumed by lower-income or single parent households, for example, then trade-driven changes in prices may increase inequality.

Tariffs rates in New Zealand are generally low. Imports of primary or manufactured products face an average tariff of 2.3%. The stylised simulation increases the tariff rate significantly. An increase in tariff rates to 25% in the model results in a rise in consumer prices on almost all commodities in New Zealand (Figure 1.25). On average, consumer prices of goods and services increase by 8.2% in the simulation. Prices on manufactured goods increase by 13.7%, with computers and electronics increasing the most in this category (17.6%). Consumer prices on food products increase on average by 9.6%, with a broad range within the category. Bovine meat products increase by 8.8% while the price of processed rice rises by 18.3%. The price of transport services by air, water, and other modes rise on average by 13.2%.

The degree to which households are exposed to a tariff increase will depend on how much they consume of each commodity.[24] For all households, a large part of household expenditure is allocated to non-tradable items, in particular housing, which represents almost 30% of total expenditure. The same is true when examining expenditure share by household composition (Figure 1.26, Panel A). Housing expenses account for 21.3% (Couple with other child(ren) only) to 41.7% (One parent with dependent child(ren) only) of total spending. Second to housing expenses, food and beverages also account for large share of total household expenditure (18.6% across all household types and ranging from 16.2% for a one person household to 21.4% for multi-family households). Households with multiple-adults spend a large share of their total expenditure on transport purchases, e.g. cars and fuel (around 15% of total expenditure), whereas transport accounts for only 8% total expenditures of a one-parent household. Beyond basic living expenses, couples without children spend the most on restaurants and hotels and transportation services (6.8% and 6.2% of total expenditure respectively), while single-parent households with dependent children spend the least on these items (2.4% and 3.2% respectively). Distributional differences are even more prominent when expenditure is expressed relative to income (Figure 1.26, Panel B), since lower income groups, in particular those households where only one member earns a wage, spend a larger share of their income and have a lower propensity to save. In New Zealand, a one-parent household with one or more dependent children spends 88.3% of their income. A one-person household spends about three-quarters of their earnings, while a couple with no children spends only 67.9% of their income. Given the role of household savings for expenditure patterns, income and expenditure-based approaches are likely to deliver different distributional effects of changes in consumer prices.

Figure 1.25. Change in consumer prices in New Zealand

Percentage

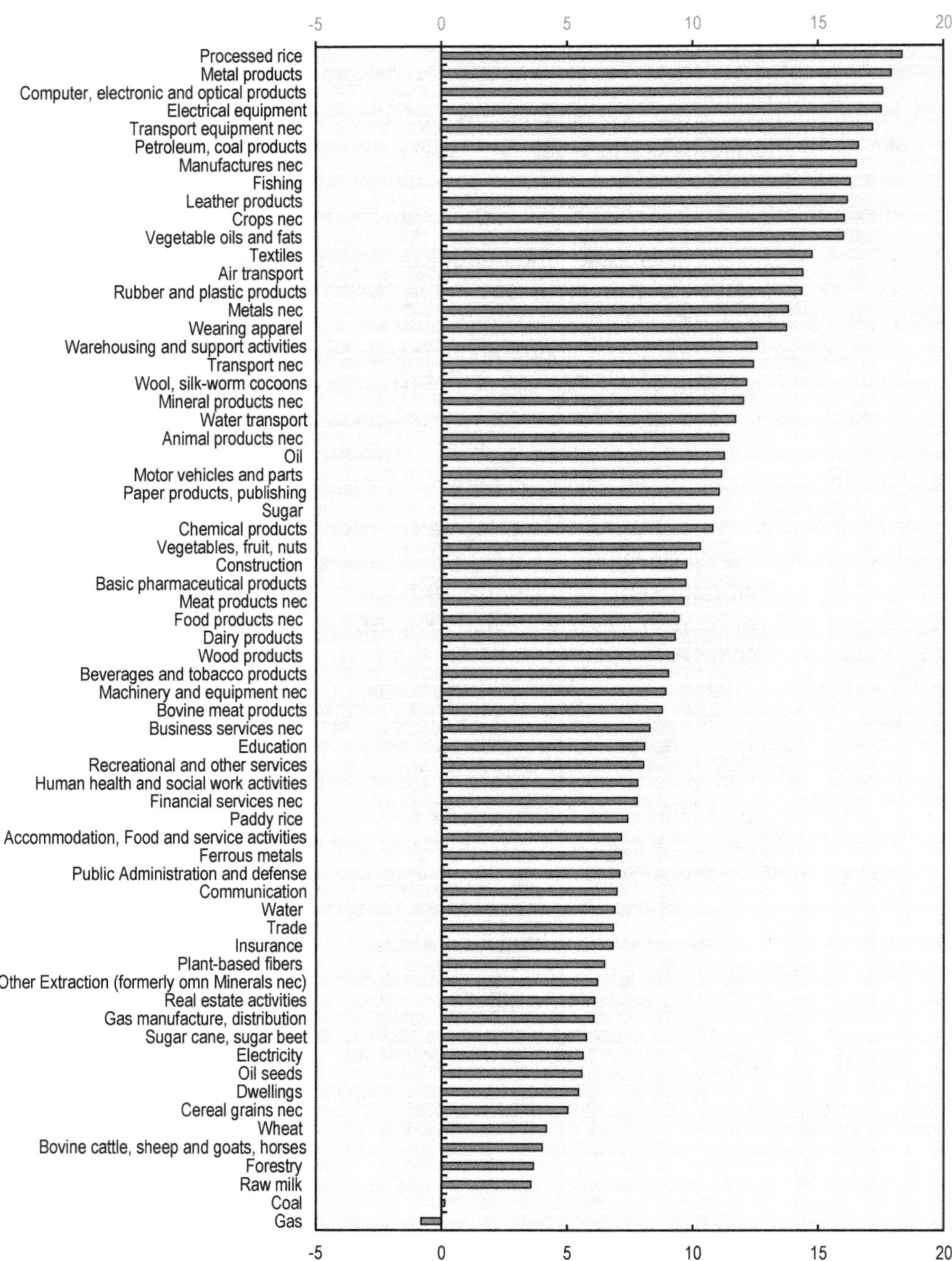

Note: This figure shows the percentage change in consumer prices in New Zealand associated with an increase in tariffs on all imports to 25% by New Zealand on all trade partners excluding Australia. The relative price changes produced by the METRO model were converted to absolute price using the exchange rate appreciation. As with most CGE models, METRO produces price changes relative to each country's numeraire, the consumer price index (CPI). With CPI fixed and normalised to one in each region, the exchange rate in the model captures the price adjustment needed in domestic relative prices to balance the external accounts. The conversion preserves the price ratios of the domestic system and maps it into international purchasing power.
Source: OECD METRO Model.

Figure 1.26. Expenditure shares by household composition

Panel A. Expenditure per category as a share of total expenditure, by household composition

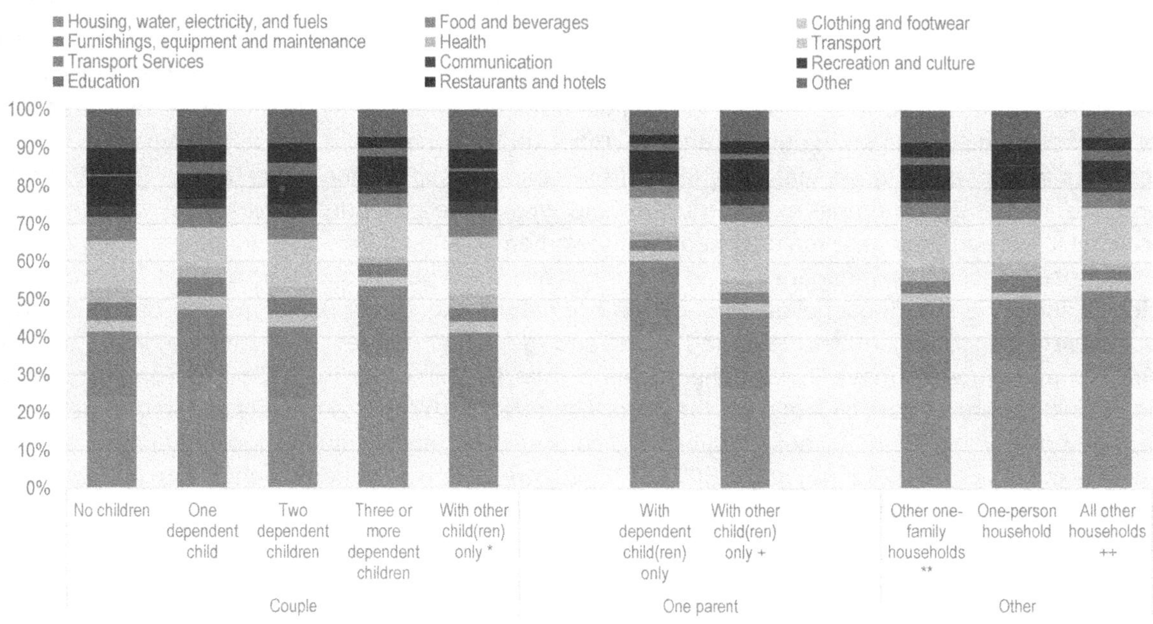

Panel B. Expenditure per category as a share of total income, by household composition

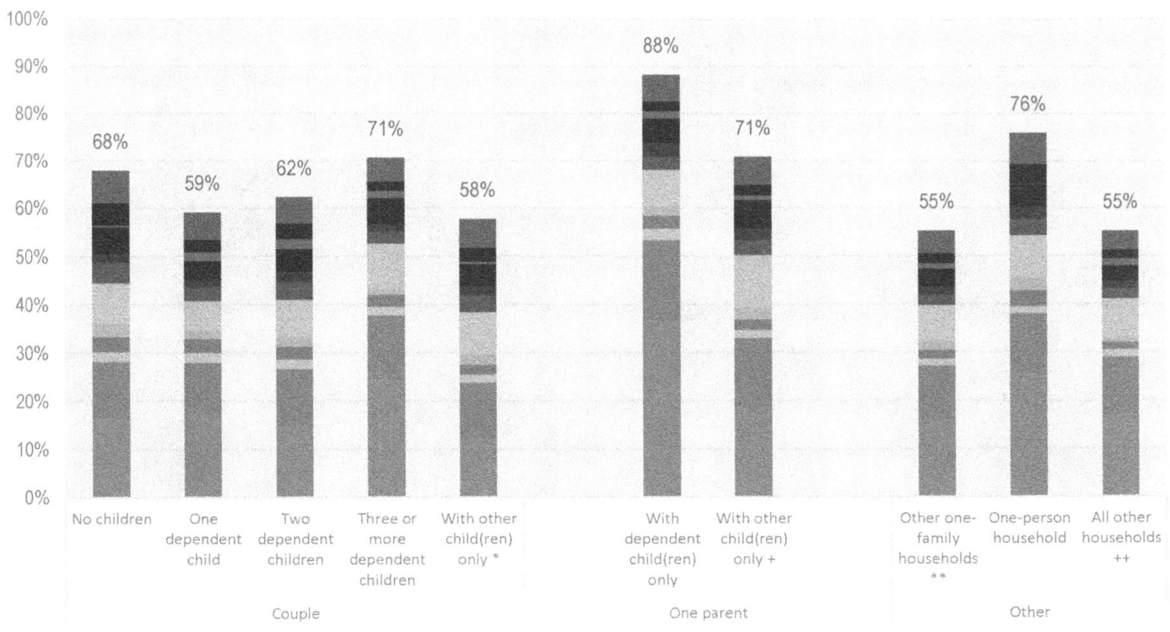

Note: OECD calculations based on New Zealand 2019 Household Economic Survey. Average weekly household expenditure as a share of total expenditure (Panel A) or share of average household weekly income (Panel B).
* Includes couple with adult children only, as well as couple with adult and dependent children.
+ Includes one parent with adult children only, as well as one parent with dependent and adult children.
** Contains all one-family households where 'other people' are present, who may be related or unrelated to the family nucleus.
++ This category is an aggregation of two-family household, three-or-more-family households, or any other multi-person households.
Source: 2019 Household Economic Survey (HES) of New Zealand.

The change in household purchasing power,[25] following the imposition of the tariff is computed both on an expenditure and on an income-based approach and presented in Figure 1.27. A unilateral increase in tariff rates on all imports of goods and services to 25% would generate a loss of 9.3% in household purchasing power on average in all households on an expenditure basis. Because New Zealand households save around 37% of their income, the purchasing power loss on an income-basis is not as pronounced but still negative nonetheless (-5.8%). On an expenditure basis, differences in the extent to which different types of households are exposed to trade-driven prices changes are small. All types of households lose about 9% of purchasing power on an expenditure basis. However, because some household types have higher propensities to consume, those that save less of their income experience larger losses from the trade-driven price increases. The most exposed household type is the one-parent household with dependent children, which are in their vast majority headed by women. The tariff increase would generate a loss of 7.8% for those households, measured on an income basis. The type of household that is the second most affected is single person households (who lose 6.8 of purchasing power on an income basis). Although these households comprise people of all ages and genders, women predominate in older single households and generally have lower pensions as compared with older men. Couples-only households spend a lower share of their income, so they are less affected by the tariff increase and experience a purchasing power loss of 6.4%. These findings are consistent with other studies looking at the distribution effects of taxes. Luu et al. (2020[11]) and OECD/KIPF (2014[13]) both found neutral effects on an expenditure basis and regressive effects on an income basis in OECD countries.

Figure 1.27. Change in purchasing power by household composition

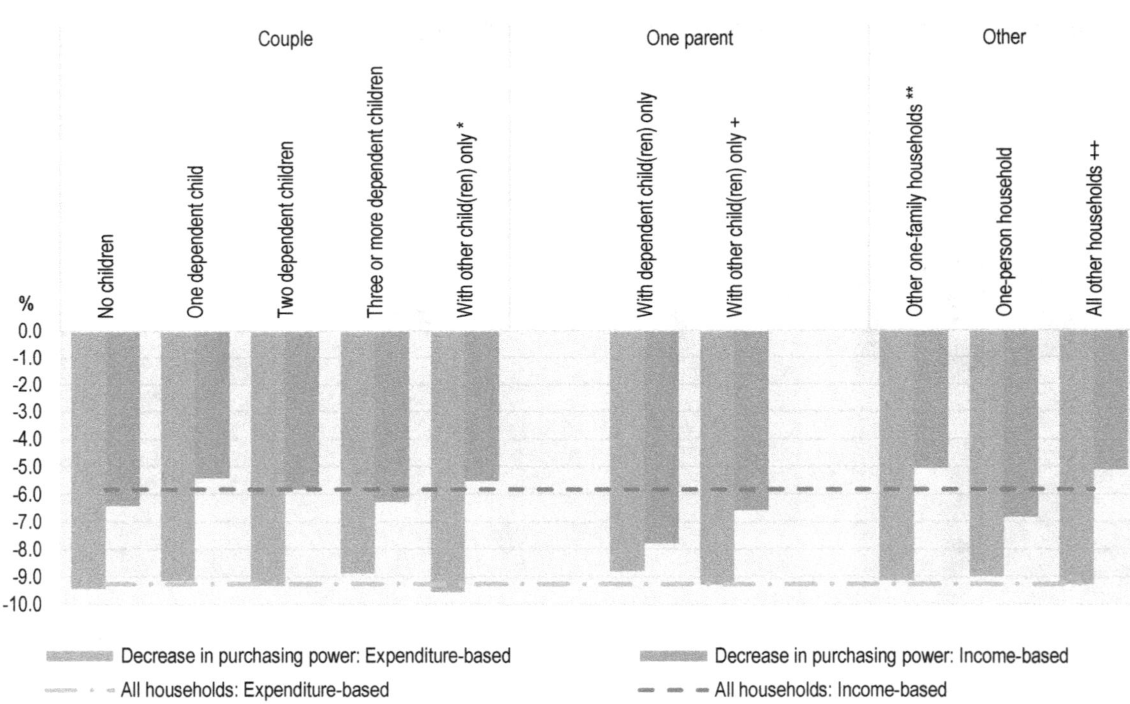

Notes

* Includes couple with adult children only, as well as couple with adult and dependent children.

\+ Includes one parent with adult children only, as well as one parent with dependent and adult children.

** Contains all one-family households where 'other people' are present who may be related or unrelated to the family nucleus.

++ This category is an aggregation of two-family households, three-or-more-family households, or any other multi-person households.

Source: OECD METRO Model and New Zealand 2019 Household Economic Survey.

The simulation implemented in this study increases import tariffs to ascertain their price impact on household expenditures, and allows conclusions to be drawn on the reverse effect. This analysis suggests that lower prices due to trade positively impact households that are made up of a single parent with dependent children even more than households with two or more adults. Since women head the vast majority of those households, they particularly benefit from the lower prices that trade brings. Another household type that benefits particularly from lower prices is one-person households. Although this study does not differentiate households by age, women commonly predominate among older single person households. These findings suggest therefore that more vulnerable household types benefit more, measured on an income basis, from lower prices. Prices of some staple foods, such as processed rice and vegetable oils, are particularly strongly affected by potential trade barriers in New Zealand.

The policy conclusion that can be reached from this analysis corroborates New Zealand's policy choices of low tariff rates and willingness to engage in trade agreements and multilateral trade negotiations. It suggests that lower tariffs can benefit more vulnerable households, where women are predominantly found. From a consumption perspective therefore, trade can serve to decrease inequality between households. It should be kept in mind, however, that a large share of household expenditure is in non-tradables, such as housing, which are not directly affected by lower prices through trade. Housing in particular accounts for a large share of expenditure, especially by single-parent households with dependent children (41%) so trade can be only one part of a suite of policies to support vulnerable households' purchasing power.

Consumption of specific products destined for women

Compared with some other countries, New Zealand maintains few tariffs on imported goods and there is limited evidence of a gender bias within those tariffs. One of the product categories where tariffs are applied is clothing. A 10% tariff is applied to both men's and women's clothing, suggesting equal trade barriers to these products. However, the absolute impact is uneven, with the value of women's clothing imports (and subsequent share of tariff revenue on these products) 47% higher than men's clothing imports. This is due to women spending more on clothing and consuming a larger share of imported clothing than men. The second area where gender-specific tariffs can be identified is on some female sanitary products. The weighted average MFN tariff on these imported products is 0.38%. In 2019, New Zealand women paid just under NZD 100 000 in tariffs for these products. While a tariff is in place for these goods, they are typically granted zero duty concession if this is requested by the importing firm.

Annex 1.A. Analysis of distributional implications of trade impacts on consumer prices

Annex Table 1.A.1. Product groups used in METRO analysis of distributional implications of trade impacts on consumer prices

Product group	Detailed products included in aggregate
Food and beverages	Bread and cereals
Food and beverages	Meat
Food and beverages	Fruit
Food and beverages	Vegetables
Food and beverages	Food products n.e.c.
Food and beverages	Coffee, tea and cocoa
Food and beverages	Mineral waters, soft drinks, fruit and vegetable juices
Food and beverages	Spirits
Food and beverages	Wine
Food and beverages	Beer
Food and beverages	Tobacco
Clothing and footwear	Clothing materials
Clothing and footwear	Garments
Clothing and footwear	Cleaning, repair and hire of clothing
Clothing and footwear	Shoes and other footwear
Clothing and footwear	Repair and hire of footwear
Housing, water, electricity, and fuels	Actual rentals paid by tenants
Housing, water, electricity, and fuels	Other actual rentals
Housing, water, electricity, and fuels	Imputed rentals of owner-occupiers
Housing, water, electricity, and fuels	Materials for the maintenance and repair of the dwelling
Housing, water, electricity, and fuels	Services for the maintenance and repair of the dwelling
Housing, water, electricity, and fuels	Water supply
Housing, water, electricity, and fuels	Refuse collection
Housing, water, electricity, and fuels	Other services relating to the dwelling n.e.c.
Housing, water, electricity, and fuels	Electricity
Housing, water, electricity, and fuels	Gas
Housing, water, electricity, and fuels	Liquid fuels
Housing, water, electricity, and fuels	Solid fuels
Housing, water, electricity, and fuels	Heat energy
Furnishings, equipment and maintenance	Furniture and furnishings
Furnishings, equipment and maintenance	Carpets and other floor coverings
Furnishings, equipment and maintenance	Repair of furniture, furnishings and floor coverings
Furnishings, equipment and maintenance	Household textiles
Furnishings, equipment and maintenance	Major household appliances whether electric or not
Furnishings, equipment and maintenance	Small electric household appliances
Furnishings, equipment and maintenance	Repair of household appliances
Furnishings, equipment and maintenance	Glassware, tableware and household utensils
Furnishings, equipment and maintenance	Major tools and equipment
Furnishings, equipment and maintenance	Small tools and miscellaneous accessories
Furnishings, equipment and maintenance	Non-durable household goods
Furnishings, equipment and maintenance	Domestic services and household services
Health	Pharmaceutical products
Health	Other medical products
Health	Therapeutic appliances and equipment
Health	Medical services
Health	Dental services

Product group	Detailed products included in aggregate
Health	Paramedical services
Health	Hospital services
Transport	Motor cars
Transport	Motor cycles
Transport	Bicycles
Transport	Spare parts and accessories for personal transport equipment
Transport	Fuels and lubricants for personal transport equipment
Transport	Other services in respect of personal transport equipment
Transport services	Passenger transport by railway
Transport services	Passenger transport by road
Transport services	Passenger transport by air
Transport services	Passenger transport by sea and inland waterway
Transport services	Combined passenger transport
Transport services	Other purchased transport services
Transport services	Postal services
Communication	Telephone and telefax equipment
Communication	Telephone and telefax services
Recreation & culture	Equipment for the reception, recording and reproduction of sound and pictures
Recreation & culture	Information processing equipment
Recreation & culture	Recording media
Recreation & culture	Repair of audio-visual, photographic and information processing equipment
Recreation & culture	Major durables for outdoor recreation
Recreation & culture	Games, toys and hobbies
Recreation & culture	Equipment for sport, camping and open-air recreation
Recreation & culture	Gardens, plants and flowers
Recreation & culture	Pets and related products
Recreation & culture	Veterinary and other services for pets
Recreation & culture	Recreational and sporting services
Recreation & culture	Cultural services
Recreation & culture	Games of chance
Recreation & culture	Books
Recreation & culture	Newspapers and periodicals
Recreation & culture	Miscellaneous printed matter
Recreation & culture	Stationery and drawing materials
Education	Pre-primary and primary education
Education	Secondary education
Education	Tertiary education
Education	Education not definable by level
Restaurants & hotels	Restaurants, cafs and the like
Restaurants & hotels	Accommodation services
Other	Hairdressing salons and personal grooming establishments
Other	Electric appliances for personal care
Other	Other appliances, articles and products for personal care
Other	Prostitution
Other	Jewellery, clocks and watches
Other	Other personal effects
Other	Life insurance
Other	Insurance connected with the dwelling
Other	Insurance connected with health
Other	Insurance connected with transport
Other	Other insurance
Other	Other financial services n.e.c.
Other	Other services n.e.c.

References

American Express (2019), *The 2019 State of Women-Owned Businesses Report*, https://about.americanexpress.com/sites/americanexpress.newshq.businesswire.com/files/doc_library/file/2019-state-of-women-owned-businesses-report.pdf. [3]

Baily, P. and D. Ford (2018), "Estimating New Zealand's tradable and non-tradable sectors using Input-Output Tables", *New Zealand Ministry for Foreign Affairs and Trade Working Paper*, Vol. December, http://, https://www.mfat.govt.nz/assets/Trade-General/Trade-stats-and-economic-research/MFAT-Working-Paper-Estimating-New-Zealands-tradable-and-non-tradable-sectors-using-Input-Output-Tables.pdf. [1]

Benz, S. and A. Jaax (2022, forthcoming), *Shedding light on drivers of services tradability over two decades*, OECD Publications, Paris. [4]

BERL (2022), *New Zealand Women in Export Trade: Understanding the barriers*, Schulze, H.; Yadav, U.; Riley, H.; Dixon, H. (Draft mimeo). [9]

Boston Consulting Group (2019), *Les inégalités d'accès au financement pénalisent les créatrices de startup: 1er barometre SISTA x BCG sur les conditions d'accès au financement des femmes dirigeant.e.s de startup*, https://static1.squarespace.com/static/5cb5f6b651f4d41671cfdd25/t/5d77bf6b1c0c795f4311284b/1568128879711/Barometre-SistaxBCG-France10sept.pdf. [10]

Deaton, A. and J. Muellbauer (1980), "An almost ideal demand system",,", *The American Economic Review*, Vol. 70/3, https://www.jstor.org/stable/1805222. [14]

Facebook (2021), *Global State of Small Business Report*, https://scontent-cdt1-1.xx.fbcdn.net/v/t39.8562-6/10000000_2773117226319503_1319481196229331970_n.pdf?_nc_cat=101&ccb=1-5&_nc_sid=ae5e01&_nc_ohc=KV41mjYRYGEAX-zGlGE&_nc_ht=scontent-cdt1-1.xx&oh=00_AT93bcp2G845hl4NRfehCFWyUmCA1Zs4cjNT3q3HXo3nWw&oe=61C044F5. [5]

Korinek, J., E. Moïsé and J. Tange (2021), "Trade and gender: A Framework of analysis", *OECD Trade Policy Papers*, No. 246, OECD Publishing, Paris, https://doi.org/10.1787/6db59d80-en. [6]

Luu, N. et al. (2020), "Mapping trade to household budget survey: A conversion framework for assessing the distributional impact of trade policies", *OECD Trade Policy Papers*, No. 244, OECD Publishing, Paris, https://doi.org/10.1787/5fc6181b-en. [11]

McKinsey Global Institute (2020), *COVID-19 and Gender Equality: Countering the Regressive Effects*, https://www.mckinsey.com/featured-insights/future-of-work/covid-19-and-gender-equality-countering-the-regressive-effects. [8]

MFAT (2022), "Inclusive and productive characteristics of New Zealand goods exporting firms", MFAT working paper, Ministry of Foreign Affairs and Trade of New Zealand, https://www.mfat.govt.nz/assets/Trade-General/Trade-stats-and-economic-research/Inclusive-and-productive-characteristics-of-New-Zealand-goods-exporting-firms-MFAT-Working-Paper.pdf. [15]

OECD (2020), "METRO Version 3 Model Documentation", [TAD/TC/WP/RD(2020)1/FINAL], https://one.oecd.org/document/TAD/TC/WP/RD(2020)1/FINAL/en/pdf. [12]

OECD/KIPF (2014), *The Distributional Effects of Consumption Taxes in OECD Countries*, OECD Tax Policy Studies, No. 22, OECD Publishing, Paris, https://doi.org/10.1787/9789264224520-en. [13]

Schneider, J. (2020), *Future of Business Survey Methodology Note*, https://scontent-cdt1-1.xx.fbcdn.net/v/t39.8562-6/238554568_111626007787616_5411963469147558965_n.pdf?_nc_cat=103&ccb=1-5&_nc_sid=ae5e01&_nc_ohc=J4wY1mDW3GIAX-Atyb7&_nc_ht=scont. [2]

Westpac New Zealand, Deloitte (2021), *Sharing the Load*, https://www.westpac.co.nz/assets/About-us/sustainability-community/documents/Sharing-the-Load-Report-2021-Westpac-NZ.pdf. [7]

Notes

[1] A full description of the LBD and IDI is available on the Stats NZ website.

[2] Disclaimer: Access to the data used in this study was provided by Stats NZ under conditions designed to give effect to the security and confidentiality provisions of the Statistics Act 1975. The results presented in this study are the work of the author, not Stats NZ or individual data suppliers. As such, they are not official statistics. They have been created for research purposes from the IDI and LBD, which are carefully managed by Stats NZ. For more information, see (MFAT, 2022[15]).

The results are based in part on tax data supplied by Inland Revenue to Stats NZ under the Tax Administration Act 1994 for statistical purposes. Any discussion of data limitations or weaknesses is in the context of using the IDI for statistical purposes, and is not related to the data's ability to support Inland Revenue's core operational requirements.

[3] For example, see Women at Work: 1991-2013 by StatsNZ (2015) for a discussion of trends in gender-based occupational segregation from 20 years of New Zealand's census data.

[4] Drilling to this level of detail entails further loss of data quality. For example, some combinations of gender, ethnicity and industry employment are suppressed by Stats NZ due to small sample size. Some interpolation of data is therefore required. However, this is not expected to materially influence the overall results. The key simplifying assumption that the export propensity by industry applies evenly still applies.

[5] This comprises: construction; health; public administration and safety; retail trade and accommodation; art, recreation and other services; education and training; financial and insurance services; rental, hiring and real estate services.

[6] See https://www.stats.govt.nz/news/gender-pay-gap-unchanged

[7] There are pockets within the health and education industries, such as aged care support, where women are paid significantly less than the average. These inequities are being addressed via the NZD 2 billion Care and Support Workers (Pay Equity) settlement.

[8] Additional information on this survey can be found at: https://datacatalog.worldbank.org/dataset/future-business-survey-aggregated-data and in Schneider (2020[2]).

[9] The analysis in the section uses the *Future of Business* survey data and should be considered as relevant to businesses with an online presence.

[10] Personal services include services such as hairdressing, wellness and other beauty treatments, laundry services, pet care and training, wedding planning, repair of computer and household goods, bicycle repair.

[11] Professional and scientific services include legal and accounting, architectural services, marketing services, design activities, photographic services and animal health care.

[12] Media, information and communication services include computer programming and consultancy, publishing activities, sound recording and music publishing, broadcasting and telecoms.

[13] The analysis in the section uses the *Future of Business* survey data and should be considered as relevant to businesses with an online presence.

[14] The survey does not specify whether customs regulations refer to the origin or destination country of the goods and services traded. Since the question refers to exports, it can be inferred that the customs regulations at issue are most likely in the destination country, i.e. in New Zealand's trading partners.

[15] The analysis in the section uses the *Future of Business* survey data and should be considered as relevant to businesses with an online presence.

[16] As a point of comparison, before the pandemic, both women and men were equally positive about their firms' prospects in June 2019 with over 60% of both women and men indicating a positive outlook for their firms. Those who had a negative view of their business's prospects were in the single digits for both women- and men-led firms in 2019.

[17] This finding was confirmed in a study of women entrepreneurs in New Zealand (BERL, 2022[9]) where women entrepreneurs that were engaged in online sales and in the technology sectors indicated that their sales and revenue had not dropped during the pandemic.

[18] This section and the following draw on information from New Zealand's firm level data sets as outlined in the *Methodology and data* section of the *Women workers* chapter above.

[19] These figures are somewhat sensitive to the leadership proxy chosen – e.g. setting the threshold at the top 10% of paid employees provides a slightly more even distribution.

[20] Refers to equity raised by start-up firms by gender of founder(s) in Crunchbase and Dealroom databases. Firms included in the analysis were those that declared residence in New Zealand, and for which information was available on the gender of the leader/founder. In the case of multiple founders those with majority men (women) were classified as men (women) led, and those that had equal number of men and women were classified as mix lead. These data refer to firms that were established after year 2000. Analysis focused on funding opportunity, hence only included venture capital (seed, pre-seed, angel, series A-Z, growth funding, late stage funding) and grants which had the amount of equity raised. Values were converted into USD and normalised to 2005 levels. This amounts to 134 firms from 2011-2020.

[21] Standard closure assumptions apply in the simulation: governments adjust spending to maintain their pre-simulation fiscal position. The trade balance is fixed, while exchange rates are flexible. Investments are savings driven.

[22] The model database is aggregated to ten regions (New Zealand, Australia, People's Republic of China (hereafter "China"), Other Asia, ASEAN, United States, other Americas, European Union (27), the United Kingdom, and rest of the world) and 65 sectors. For the description of the sectors, see https://www.gtap.agecon.purdue.edu/databases/v10/v10_sectors.aspx#Sector65.

[23] The New Zealand Household Survey uses the New Zealand Household Expenditure Classification (NZHEC). To follow the framework described in Luu et al (2020[11]), a correspondence table between NZHEC and the Classification of Individual Consumption According to Purpose (COICOP) was produced. The correspondence table links the 65 sectors in the METRO model to 157 NZHEC product codes.

[24] See Annex Table 2.A.1 for a list of product groups covered.

[25] This book follows the approach in Luu et al (2020[11]), which computed the change in purchasing power based on the compensating variation approach (Deaton and Muellbauer, 1980[14]).

2. New Zealand's trade policy settings

Chapter 2 outlines New Zealand's trade policy settings that are of particular importance to women. It includes a review of the gender-related provisions in its trade agreements – both those that specifically mention non-discrimination and women's empowerment, and those that, although they do not specifically mention women, may most affect them. New Zealand's performance in facilitating trade is compared with that of other small, open economies: trade facilitating measures most aid small businesses, where women business owners and leaders are disproportionately represented. This chapter also includes an overview of New Zealand's barriers to trade in services sectors, where women work most.

This chapter will examine New Zealand's trade policy settings in several areas of particular importance for women. The chapter will begin with a survey of the gender-related provisions in New Zealand's trade agreements, both those that refer to gender and women explicitly, and those that are of particular importance to women although they are not explicitly targeted by the provisions. New Zealand's trade facilitating policies are then reviewed. Women entrepreneurs are strongly impacted by trade policies that facilitate trade because they generally own and lead businesses that tend to be smaller than those owned and led by men; women also have access to less capital. The last section examines the trade restrictiveness of New Zealand's services sectors; as noted in Chapter 1, a high majority of women work and lead businesses in the services sectors.

Survey and typology of gender-related provisions in current agreements

Like most countries, New Zealand has not traditionally included specific provisions relating to women or gender equality in its trade agreements. In recent years, however, New Zealand has increasingly focussed on the gendered impacts of trade and trade rules; for instance, by having played an instrumental role in the Global Trade and Gender Arrangement (GTAGA).

There is no single definition of a "gender-related" provision in a trade agreement (Monteiro, 2018[1]). Here we consider as "gender-related" any text that acknowledges the gender-based inequalities that can be reinforced or reduced by international trade and investment, and text that offers commitment, vision, or actions to challenge such inequalities, irrespective of whether it explicitly uses the words "women" or "gender equality."[1]

Of the twelve bilateral and regional trade agreements (PTAs) that New Zealand has ratified, only three mention women explicitly: the Comprehensive and Progressive Agreement for Trans-Pacific Partnership (CPTPP), the Digital Economy Partnership Agreement (DEPA) and the NZ-Singapore Closer Economic Partnership Agreement. New Zealand-Singapore mentions women specifically only in its Preamble. New Zealand has also agreed to two non-binding international texts dedicated to trade and gender: the 2017 Buenos Aires Declaration on Trade and Women's Economic Empowerment and the 2020 Global Trade and Gender Arrangement.

The gender-related content of New Zealand's trade agreements is summarised in Table 2.1. This chapter will survey explicit gender-related provisions in New Zealand's trade agreements before considering implicit gender-related provisions.

Table 2.1. Gender-related provisions in New Zealand's trade agreements

Date	Agreement	Explicit gender-related provision	Refers to international gender-related standard	SMEs	Labour Standards	Inclusive Development	Redressing Inequalities	Right to regulate	Other provisions favourable to women
1980 (& 1981)	South Pacific Regional Trade and Economic Cooperation Agreement (SPARTECA)			I			I		
2000 (& 2018)	New Zealand - Singapore Closer Economic Partnership	X (2018 Upgrade Preamble)						I	I

Date	Agreement	Explicit gender-related provision	Refers to international gender-related standard	SMEs	Labour Standards	Inclusive Development	Redressing Inequalities	Right to regulate	Other provisions favourable to women
2005	Thailand - New Zealand (NZ-Thailand Closer Economic Partnership Agreement)			I			I	I	
2005 (& 2006)	Trans-Pacific Strategic Economic Partnership (P4) (Brunei Darussalam, Chile, Singapore, and New Zealand)			I	I		I	I	
2008 (& 2021)	China – New Zealand		I	I	[M] I+			I	I
2009 (& 2010)	ASEAN - Australia - New Zealand (Brunei Darussalam, Cambodia, Indonesia, Laos, Malaysia, Myanmar, Singapore, Thailand, Viet Nam, the Philippines and New Zealand and Australia) (AANZFTA)			I	[M] I	I	I		
2009 (& 2010)	New Zealand - Malaysia			I	I		I	I	
2010 (& 2011)	Hong Kong, China - New Zealand (NZ-Hong Kong, China Closer Economic Partnership)				[M] I	I		I	
2015	NZ-Korea Free Trade Agreement		I+ (ILO 1998 and 2008 Declarations)	I	I+	I		I	I
2018	Comprehensive and Progressive Agreement for Trans-Pacific Partnership (CPTPP)	X	I+(SDGs) ILO	I	X	X	I	I	
2017	Pacific Agreement		I+ (ILO)		I	I	I	I	I

Date	Agreement	Explicit gender-related provision	Refers to international gender-related standard	SMEs	Labour Standards	Inclusive Development	Redressing Inequalities	Right to regulate	Other provisions favourable to women
(& 2020)	on Closer Economic Relations Plus (PACER US)								
2020	Digital Economy Partnership Agreement (New Zealand, Chile, Singapore) (DEPA)	X	I+ (SDGs)	I	I	X	I	I	
2020 (2022)	Regional Comprehensive Economic Partnership (RCEP)			I				I	
TBA	New Zealand – United Kingdom Free Trade Agreement (NZ-UK FTA)	X	I+ (ILO)	I	X	X	X	I	
2017	Buenos Aires Joint Declaration on Trade and Women's Economic Empowerment	X	X (SDG5, CEDAW)	X		X	X		NA
2020	Global Trade and Gender Arrangement (GTAGA)	X	X (SDG5; CEDAW; Buenos Aires Declaration; ILO)	X	X	X	X		NA
2021	Reference Paper on Services Domestic Regulation	X						I	

Note: [M] Memorandum of Understanding or side-agreement on Labour signed in parallel to the trade agreement; I Implicit gender-related provision; I+ Explicit reference to a text that implicitly protects women's rights; X Explicit gender-related provision. ASEAN includes Brunei Darussalam, Cambodia, Indonesia, Laos, Malaysia, Myanmar, Singapore, Thailand, Viet Nam, and the Philippines. Trans-Pacific Strategic Economic Partnership (P4) includes Brunei Darussalam, Chile, Singapore, and New Zealand. Digital Economy Partnership Agreement (DEPA) includes New Zealand, Chile, and Singapore.
* 2018 Upgrade Preamble.
** ILO 1998 & 2008 Declarations.
*** SDG5; CEDAW; Buenos Aires Declaration; ILO. "Right to regulate" provisions are those meant to ensure that domestic gender-supportive policies are sheltered from dispute under the agreement.
Source: The authors, based on the text of the relevant agreements.

Agreements with explicit gender-related provisions

New Zealand – United Kingdom Free Trade Agreement (NZ-UK FTA)

New Zealand and the United Kingdom reached agreement on the key elements of a new FTA in October 2021. The Agreement in Principle (AIP) commits to including in the FTA a dedicated chapter that will advance women's economic empowerment and promote gender equality in trade.[2] This chapter will be supplemented by a number of gender equality provisions agreed across the FTA. Commitments in the trade and gender equality chapter will include:

- Provisions to implement the obligations under existing international agreements and instruments that New Zealand and the United Kingdom have signed up to and which address women's rights or gender equality.
- Commitments on cooperative activities that aim to enhance the ability of women to benefit from the FTA and address barriers for women in trade such as lack of access to markets, business and leadership networks, and finance. Future cooperation may focus on promoting financial inclusion, building trade-related capacity and enhancing skills of women at work, in business and at senior levels, fostering women's entrepreneurship, and supporting economic opportunities for diverse groups of women in trade and investment, including wāhine Māori.
- A commitment to develop a framework for analysing sex or gender-disaggregated data, and gender-focused analysis of trade policies.
- In addition to the Trade and Gender chapter, gender-related provisions will be incorporated in the Labour and Trade and Development chapters. The Labour chapter affirms obligations as members of the ILO and will include provisions with respect to women's equality in the workplace.

Comprehensive and Progressive Agreement for Trans-Pacific Partnership (CPTPP)

The CPTPP contains two explicit references to women. One is in its Labour chapter, which notes that Parties "shall, as appropriate leverage their respective membership in regional and multilateral fora to further their common interests in addressing labour issues," identifying amongst areas for cooperation, promotion of equality of, elimination of discrimination against, and the employment interests of women.[3]

The second reference is in the Development chapter, which contains a specific article on Women and Economic Growth.[4] In this, CPTPP Parties "recognise that enhancing opportunities in their territories for women, including workers and business owners, to participate in the domestic and global economy contributes to economic development." The Parties further recognise the benefit of sharing experiences "in designing, implementing and strengthening programmes to encourage this participation." The article sets out the types of cooperative activities that Parties "shall consider undertaking." These include providing advice or training and exchanging information and experience on programmes aimed at helping women build their skills and capacity, enhancing their access to markets, technology and financing, developing women's leadership networks, and identifying best practices related to workplace flexibility.

The agreement also includes various provisions that, although worded in a gender-neutral way, may help advance gender equality or help women in CPTPP economies to trade more successfully. Some of its implicit gender-related provisions in CPTPP are presented in Section 3.1.2. More generally, as it addresses regulatory barriers – with a strong emphasis on non-tariff barriers (NTBs) such as procedural obstacles or opaque technical regulations– the CPTPP can be viewed as supportive of women given that the burden of many NTBs falls disproportionately heavily on women entrepreneurs and SMEs as a result of the high fixed costs involved (Honey, 2018[2]).

When they signed the CPTPP, New Zealand, Canada and Chile adopted a Declaration on Progressive and Inclusive Trade. Through this they agreed to work together to examine the effectiveness of the CPTPP with respect to sustainable development, gender, SMEs and labour rights, within three years of the entry into force of CPTPP.[5]

Digital Economy Partnership Agreement (DEPA)

The Digital Economy Partnership Agreement was signed by New Zealand, Chile and Singapore in June 2020. DEPA integrates gender provisions in a number of ways. Its Preamble reaffirms the importance of promoting public interest goals such as gender equality, labour rights and inclusive trade. Its article on digital inclusion acknowledges the value of ensuring that "all people and businesses have what they need to participate in, contribute to, and benefit from the digital economy". It stipulates that Parties shall cooperate on matters relating to digital inclusion, including participation of women, rural populations, Indigenous Peoples and more vulnerable groups, and sets out possible ways of cooperating such as addressing barriers in accessing opportunities afforded by the digital economy and sharing best practices with respect to digital inclusion.

Buenos Aires Declaration on Trade and Women's Economic Empowerment

WTO Members which have endorsed the Buenos Aires Declaration agree to collaborate on making their trade and development policies more gender-responsive, acknowledging that international trade and investment are engines of economic growth. They acknowledge the need to develop evidence-based interventions to address barriers that limit opportunities for women in the economy.

The Declaration sets out a number of activities to this end: sharing experiences relating to policies and programs to encourage women's participation nationally and internationally; sharing best practices for conducting gender-based analysis of trade policies and for the monitoring of their effects; sharing methods and procedures for collecting and analysing gender-disaggregated data and monitoring and evaluation methodologies; working together in the WTO to remove barriers to women's economic empowerment and increase their participation in trade; and ensuring that Aid for Trade supports the analysis, design and implementation of more gender-responsive trade policies. In its Preamble, the Declaration recalls SDG5, covering the achievement of gender equality and empowerment of all women and girls, and reaffirms signatories' commitment to implement the obligations under the Convention on the Elimination of all Forms of Discrimination Against Women (CEDAW).

The Buenos Aires Declaration created a mandate within the WTO for further work on gender equality and on trade and women's economic empowerment, which has been mainly undertaken through the Informal Working Group on Trade and Gender established in 2020. New Zealand co-sponsored the follow up declaration, although this has not yet been launched due to the postponement of the Twelfth WTO Ministerial Conference.

Global Trade and Gender Arrangement (GTAGA)

As an instrument dedicated wholly to trade and gender, GTAGA contains many explicit references to gender equality, women's economic empowerment and women's participation in the economy. Its Preamble (General Understandings) recalls SDG 5, notes that it is inappropriate to derogate from gender equality laws and regulations to encourage trade or investment, and acknowledges the need to identify the range of barriers that limit opportunities for women in the economy and deliver evidence-based interventions in response.

In its operative provisions, Participants reaffirm their commitments under CEDAW and "any other international agreement addressing women's rights or gender equality to which they are party" and acknowledge the CEDAW Committee's general recommendations. They also agree to implement the Buenos Aires Declaration.

GTAGA's General Dispositions specify the purposes of the "mutually supportive trade and gender policies" to which Participants agree. These are to improve women's access to economic opportunities to further women's economic empowerment and sustainable development, to improve and increase women's participation in trade and investment, to enforce signatories' laws and regulations promoting gender equality and avoid encouraging trade and investment by weakening or reducing protections for women.

GTAGA sets out specific provisions on gender and trade in services, gender and responsible business conduct and discrimination in the workplace. It provides that Participants will share experiences relating to policies and programmes to encourage women's full and equal participation. Participants also commit to report on progress under the WTO Trade Policy Review Mechanism. Similar to the gender chapters in recent bilateral trade agreements between Canada, Chile, Brazil and others,[6] it sets out means of cooperation and non-exhaustive lists of areas for cooperation, including supporting economic opportunities for Indigenous women. GTAGA creates a Trade and Gender Working Group and mandates that a Contact Point for Trade and Gender be set up in each of the Parties. A first periodic review of the Arrangement is due to take place within three years.

WTO Reference Paper on Services Domestic Regulation

In 2021, a group of WTO Members adopted new rules with a view to clarifying and harmonising the processes by which countries regulate authorisation of foreign service suppliers. These rules – set out in the Reference Paper – cover licensing and qualification requirements and procedures as well as technical standards. They include a provision on non-discrimination between men and women: the first of its kind to be included in a WTO text (World Trade Organization, 2021[3]). The provision stipulates that if a Member adopts or maintains measures relating to the authorisation for the supply of a service, the Member shall ensure that such measures do not discriminate between men and women. Significantly, the Reference Paper specifies that "[d]ifferential treatment that is reasonable and objective, and aims to achieve a legitimate purpose, and adoption by Members of temporary special measures aimed at accelerating de facto equality between men and women, shall not be considered discrimination for the purposes of this provision."

Implicit gender-related provisions in trade agreements

Trade agreements prior to 2017 were generally drafted with no explicit reference to the fact that men and women participate in, and are affected by, trade in different ways.[7] Nonetheless, for the purposes of this *Review*, the texts of all New Zealand's PTAs have been examined to glean whether any of their provisions might implicitly be favourable to women. Those provisions that are most relevant to women are presented here under five headings: (1) SMEs, (2) labour standards, (3 inclusive development, (4) redressing inequalities, and (5) the right to regulate.

Provisions in favour of SMEs

Most of New Zealand's trade agreements acknowledge that SMEs need special assistance to benefit from international trade. For instance, the Investment Chapter of the 2005 New Zealand-Thailand agreement notes "capacity building, including for small and medium enterprises" as one of the areas in which the Parties may strengthen and develop cooperation efforts. As Table 2 indicates, the attention paid to SMEs' has increased over time, with the more recent agreements containing dedicated chapters on the topic. None of New Zealand's PTAs explicitly make the link between SMEs and gender equality or women's economic empowerment, but GTAGA does.

The Regional Comprehensive Economic Partnership Agreement (RCEP) has no reference to gender equality or women. It does however have a chapter on SMEs.8 CPTPP, in addition to its explicit gender-related provisions, includes a dedicated chapter on SMEs.9 SME chapters' contents may particularly benefit women. Both RCEP's and CPTPP's provide for information sharing and cooperation to enable SMEs to benefit from the agreement. RCEP's SME chapter requires each Party to establish a Contact Point to "facilitate cooperation and information sharing under this Chapter." CPTPP goes further in that it sets up a formal intergovernmental SME Committee to cooperate on, and share experiences regarding, support for SMEs.

Other RCEP and CPTPP chapters also address the needs of SMEs. One example is RCEP's chapter on economic and technical cooperation says that the Parties shall explore and undertake cooperation activities, including capacity building and technical assistance that focus on small and medium enterprises.

CPTPP's chapters on Government Procurement[10] and on Cooperation and Capacity-Building recognise respectively the importance of facilitating the participation of SMEs and that SMEs may require assistance in participating in global markets. Of these three chapters, only the one on government procurement is subject to the CPTPP dispute settlement mechanism. DEPA also contains a section on trade and investment opportunities for SMEs in the digital economy.

Other RCEP and CPTPP chapters also address the needs of SMEs. One example is RCEP's chapter on economic and technical cooperation says that the Parties shall explore and undertake cooperation activities, including capacity building and technical assistance that focus on small and medium enterprises. CPTPP's chapters on Government Procurement[11] and on Cooperation and Capacity-Building[12] recognise respectively the importance of facilitating the participation of SMEs and that SMEs may require assistance in participating in global markets. Of these three chapters, only the one on government procurement is subject to the CPTPP dispute settlement mechanism. DEPA also contains a section on trade and investment opportunities for SMEs in the digital economy.

Labour standards

All New Zealand PTAs adopted since 2005 include at least some reference to labour standards – most referring to the need to cooperate in this area. Some of these references are contained in the text itself, some in labour side-agreements or Memorandi of Understanding (MoUs). The more recent PTAs refer to Parties' obligations as members of the ILO and/or the 1998 ILO Declaration on Fundamental Principles and Rights at Work[13] (ILO Declaration), one of the principles of which is to eliminate discrimination in respect of employment and occupation.

Some agreements – e.g. PACER Plus – cite the need to avoid lowering labour (and other) standards to attract investment or increase trade and some specify that labour standards should not be used to disguise otherwise protectionist measures. CPTPP further specifies that no Party shall fail to effectively enforce its labour laws "through a sustained or recurring course of action or inaction in a manner affecting trade or investment between the Parties after the date of entry into force of this Agreement."[14] Several agreements mandate cooperation on labour-related issues.

CPTPP's Labour Chapter mandates Parties to "...leverage their respective membership in regional and multilateral fora to further their common interests in addressing labour issues." It also includes a provision requiring Parties to endeavour to encourage enterprises to voluntarily adopt corporate social responsibility initiatives on labour issues that have been endorsed or are supported by that Party.[15] The chapter sets up a cooperative labour dialogue and a Labour Council composed of senior government representatives. Disputes under the labour chapter are subject to the CPTPP dispute settlement mechanism.

Inclusive development

New Zealand's PTAs have only very recently started mentioning inclusive economic growth or development (Table 2.1). Prior to these, one has referenced the objective of sustainable development (AANZFTA) and two have acknowledged that economic development and social development are interdependent (NZ-Hong Kong China Closer Economic Partnership, PACER Plus).

CPTPP goes further. In reaffirming the importance of inclusive trade,[16] its Preamble indirectly acknowledges the need to pay heed to vulnerable groups. Further, Article 23.1.2 of the Development chapter states that "The Parties acknowledge the importance of development in promoting inclusive economic growth...". Other parts of the Development Chapter recognise the potential for joint development activities between the Parties "to reinforce efforts to achieve sustainable development goals".

Redressing inequalities

Treaty provisions that seek to provide training, facilitate information sharing, or develop business networks may benefit women particularly. Most New Zealand PTAs provide for some form of cooperation on capacity-building or training. None of the agreements note priority to women or suggest gender balance, but these gender-neutral provisions may be especially valuable for women. CPTPP's Development Chapter, for instance, recognises that generating and sustaining broad-based economic growth requires sustained high-level commitment by CPTPP governments "to effectively and efficiently administer public institutions, invest in public infrastructure, welfare, health and education systems, and foster entrepreneurship and access to economic opportunity". Article 23.5 on Education, Science and Technology, Research and Innovation recognises that promotion and development of education, science and technology, research and innovation can play an important role in accelerating growth, enhancing competitiveness, creating jobs, and expanding trade and investment among the Parties.

Right to regulate

"Right to regulate" provisions are meant to ensure that domestic gender-supportive policies are sheltered from dispute under the agreement. These can take the form of exemptions and reservations listed by the parties to some of their PTA commitments. "Right to regulate" provisions often aim to ensure that other PTA provisions do not cause gender-positive action to backtrack, or to allay concerns about the PTA's potential to aggravate existing gender gaps (Korinek, Moïsé and Tange, 2021[4]). Most of New Zealand's PTAs have recognised governments' right to regulate to meet national policy objectives. Some provide more detail through noting the right to introduce new regulations and/or recognise the role of governments in providing and funding public services. In the NZ-Korea agreement, for example, both Korea and New Zealand reserve the right to adopt or maintain any measure with respect to a number of social services established or maintained for public purposes that may be particularly valuable to women, such as social security or insurance, social welfare, public training, public utilities, public transport, public housing, health, and child care."[17]

Trade facilitation in New Zealand

Benefits of trade facilitation for women-led businesses

Women traders are often at a disadvantage to meet the high cost and time demands of complex trading requirements since they own and manage smaller businesses than men do, and they have less time due to an increased burden of unpaid work. Trade facilitation reforms particularly benefit micro and small firms, where women entrepreneurs are disproportionately represented. Trade facilitation reforms can help everyone to trade, but particularly women business owners and leaders.

Trade facilitation reforms making border processes more efficient – as measured by the OECD Trade Facilitation Indicators (TFIs)[18] – can reduce trade costs on average for OECD countries by more than 10%. The trade facilitation policies that contribute most to reducing trade costs are the streamlining of trade procedures and formalities, the automation of border processes, and the availability of information (OECD, 2018[5]).

The automation of the border process can be particularly important for women-led micro, small and medium-sized enterprises (MSMEs), not only because it reduces the costs of processing documentation, but also because by dematerialising formalities it shelters women entrepreneurs from potential harassment and discrimination. Additionally, reforms that reduce the time required for processes can benefit women who often face additional constraints on their time related to care responsibilities. Greater transparency particularly benefits women-led businesses with fewer professional networks (Korinek, Moïsé and Tange, 2021[4]).

Moreover, measures such as the inclusion of MSMEs in consultation processes or the efficiency of appeal procedures – measures which can be associated with higher fixed costs – have a greater impact on the propensity or probability of firms to engage in exporting and importing – that is, on trade at the extensive margin. In turn, measures such as fees and charges, streamlining of procedures and automating border processes, which tend to be associated with reductions in variable costs, have a bigger impact on the export and import values of firms – trade at the intensive margin. Automation and streamlining of border processes can each support MSMEs in OECD countries to both start engaging in international trade and enhance the value of their exports and imports by up to 7.5% (López González and Sorescu, 2019[6]).

In the digital era where more small parcels cross international borders, issues such as trade facilitation have taken on greater significance. This type of trade is especially important for individuals and smaller firms, offering new opportunities to engage in trade whether as importers or exporters. When parcels cross borders, it is the role of Customs authorities and other border agencies to manage traffic. This means enforcing trade rules, such as tariffs, but also undertaking health and safety, security and quality checks. Even modest improvements in trade facilitation policies such as transparency, automation and streamlining of processes at borders, as well as border agency co-operation, are found to have a positive impact on parcel exports of between 6% and 14% (López González and Sorescu, 2021[7]). An increase in the ease of trade in parcels may affect women-owned businesses even more than those owned by men since women-owned businesses tend to export more to individuals whereas men-owned businesses export more to other businesses (Korinek, Moïsé and Tange, 2021[4]).

Trade facilitation state of play in New Zealand[19]

New Zealand exceeds or is close to worldwide best practice in the following areas covered by the OECD Trade Facilitation Indicators: information availability, involvement of trade community, appeal procedures, fees and charges, simplification and harmonisation of documents, automation of border processes, streamlining of procedures, border agency co-operation, and governance and impartiality (Figure 28).

New Zealand performs on par with other small open economies such as Denmark, Ireland and Switzerland. Economies such as Finland or Singapore perform better in some areas such as advance rulings and simplification of trade documents, but New Zealand is better or on par in areas of fees and charges and streamlining of procedures. In turn, New Zealand exceeds the performance of other small open economies such as Israel, notably in the involvement of trade community, streamlining of procedures, and border agency co-operation (Figure 2.1).

Since the conclusion of the WTO Trade Facilitation Agreement (TFA) in 2013, New Zealand improved its performance particularly in the automation and streamlining of border processes – both areas of particular importance as regards women traders – as well as domestic border agency co-operation (Figure 2.2). This progress is reflected in reductions of more than 50% in the average costs to export and import over the past decade, albeit costs and time to trade appear to remain stable over recent years.[20]

One of the areas where significant progress was made concerns the Authorised Economic Operators (AEO) programme Secure Exports Scheme. The Secure Exports Scheme currently provides for a wide range of benefits to traders that are certified AEOs, namely: deferred payment of duties, taxes, fees and charges; use of comprehensive guarantees or reduced guarantees; low rate of physical inspections; low documentary and data requirements; and rapid release time. Information on the requirements and process for certification – particularly beneficial to women traders – is also made fully available, while the time for obtaining the AEO certification has been reduced to 50 days.

Figure 2.1. Comparison of Trade Facilitation Indicators among small, open economies, 2019-20

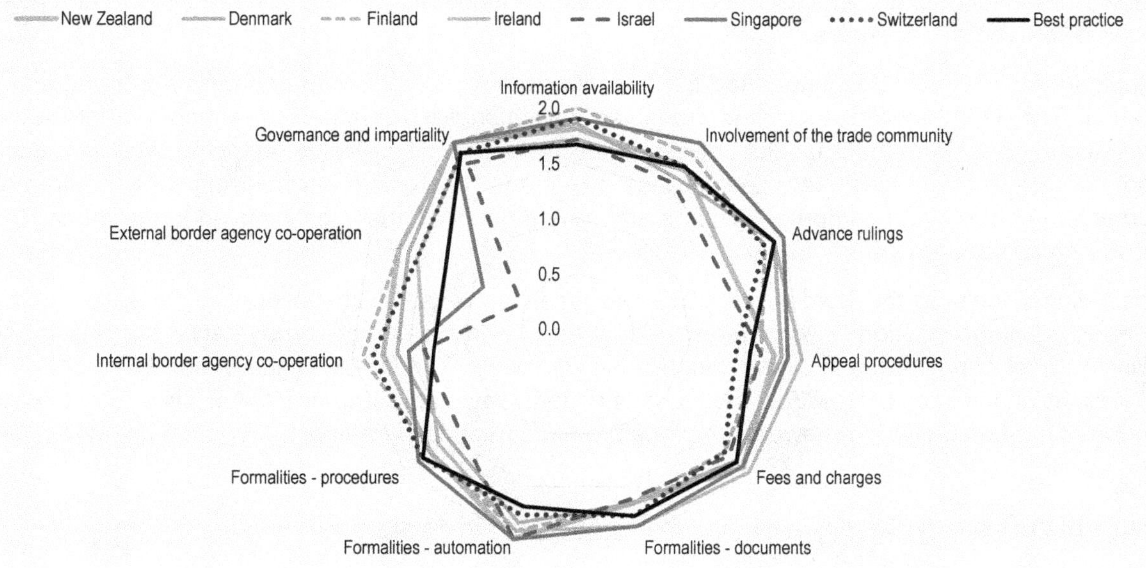

New Zealand
Denmark
Finland
Ireland
Israel
Singapore
Switzerland
Best practice
Information availability
2.0
1.5
1.0
0.5
0.0
Involvement of the trade community
Advance rulings
Appeal procedures
Fees and charges
Formalities - documents
Formalities - automation
Formalities - procedures
Internal border agency co-operation
External border agency co-operation
Governance and impartiality

Note: Each indicator goes from 0 to 2, with 2 being the best possible score. Best practice is the 25th percentile by TFI area.
Source: OECD Trade Facilitation Indicators, https://www.compareyourcountry.org/trade-facilitation.

Figure 2.2. Progress in trade facilitation performance in New Zealand since 2012

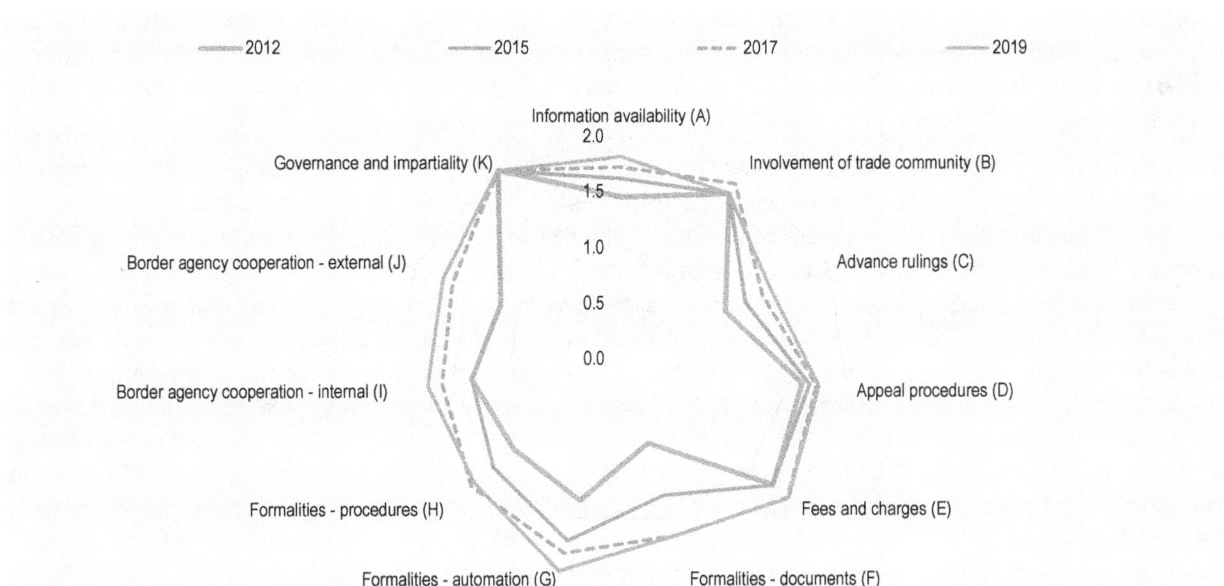

2012
2015
2017
2019
Information availability (A)
2.0
1.5
1.0
0.5
0.0
Involvement of trade community (B)
Advance rulings (C)
Appeal procedures (D)
Fees and charges (E)
Formalities - documents (F)
Formalities - automation (G)
Formalities - procedures (H)
Border agency cooperation - internal (I)
Border agency cooperation - external (J)
Governance and impartiality (K)

Note: Each indicator goes from 0 to 2, with 2 being the best possible score.
Source: OECD Trade Facilitation Indicators, https://www.compareyourcountry.org/trade-facilitation.

Among digital tools for trade facilitation, New Zealand increased the percentage of import and export declarations cleared electronically and the share of procedures that allow for electronic processing. It also made progress on the electronic exchange of documents such as certificates of origin and SPS certificates.

Significant progress has also been recorded in the implementation of the Trade Single Window (TSW), particularly as regards the legal framework and technological architecture supporting it. The Trade Single Window is an electronic channel for the cargo and excise industries to submit information to and receive responses from border agencies.[21]

Progress in the TSW has also supported the overall advances in improving domestic border agency co-operation. The TFIs highlight that New Zealand's institutionalised mechanism supporting inter-agency coordination has a permanent technical Secretariat; clear provisions for its financing; and includes the majority of relevant agencies. New Zealand has also made progress in harmonising data requirements, documentary controls and computer systems among the different agencies involved in the management of cross-border trade.

Beyond digital tools at the border, progress has been achieved in the overall digitalisation of trade processes. E-authentication, e-signatures, e-contracts, e-invoices and e-payments support today a growing number of physical and digital transactions worldwide. The OECD Digital Trade Inventory (DTI)[22] highlights that in the case of New Zealand, various regional trade agreements (RTAs) it is a party to include provisions on e-transaction frameworks, e-signatures and paperless trading.

New Zealand's regulatory environment for services trade

This chapter sheds light on trade policies and relevant domestic policies affecting New Zealand services sectors, where the majority of women work and lead businesses. The trade cost equivalent of services trade barriers largely exceeds the average tariff on traded goods and these barriers have as strong an impact on services exports as on services imports (OECD, 2020[8]).[23]

Due to the nature of services trade barriers, these do not only include laws and regulations only affecting foreign providers. To a large extent, barriers to services trade result from non-discriminatory rules and regulations behind the border. These laws and regulations do not only affect activities of foreign companies providing services in New Zealand on a cross-border basis or New Zealand affiliates of foreign multinationals, but also domestic New Zealand services companies.

At the same time, restrictive services policies not only limit the ability of services providers to access foreign markets, but also the ability of domestic firms to access services inputs at competitive prices. There is evidence that services trade barriers represent a significant cost for importers as well as exporters of services. High levels of services restrictiveness are strongly associated with low levels of services exports, which can be explained by lower competitiveness of services suppliers in highly restrictive environments (Nordås and Rouzet, 2015[9]). Also, these barriers have a strong negative impact on the value of cross-border services transactions. Expressed as percentages of total trade value, average multilateral services trade costs represent around 57% for communication services and 54% in business services, around 60% for transport services, around 103% for insurance services, and around 255% for financial services (Benz and Jaax, 2020[10]). Restrictive services policies also increase costs for firms in the manufacturing sector (Nordås and Rouzet, 2015[9]). Such cross-sectoral spillovers are a consequence of the creation of new business models where goods and services are bundled and due to the integration of services and goods in global value chains (Miroudot and Cadestin, 2017[11]).

OECD has estimated the impact of services trade barriers on trade costs for New Zealand firms. The hypothetical scenario is a unilateral reform that closes half of the gap in services trade restrictiveness between New Zealand and the most liberal country in each sector (Figure 2.3). The impact would be substantial for services that are crucial supporting activities to other sectors, such as commercial banking (where firms' trade costs would be reduced by about 20% if New Zealand closed the gap with the most liberal country by half), air transport (around 15% trade cost reduction) and cargo handling (around 13% trade cost reduction). Even for services where New Zealand is relatively close to the most liberal country, such as insurance services, there is still potential for a sizable reduction of services trade costs in the range of 6%. Lowering restrictions in these sectors would lower costs and enable trade in a wide range of goods and services sectors.

Figure 2.3. Potential services trade cost reduction in New Zealand

If New Zealand closed half of the gap with the most liberal country by sector

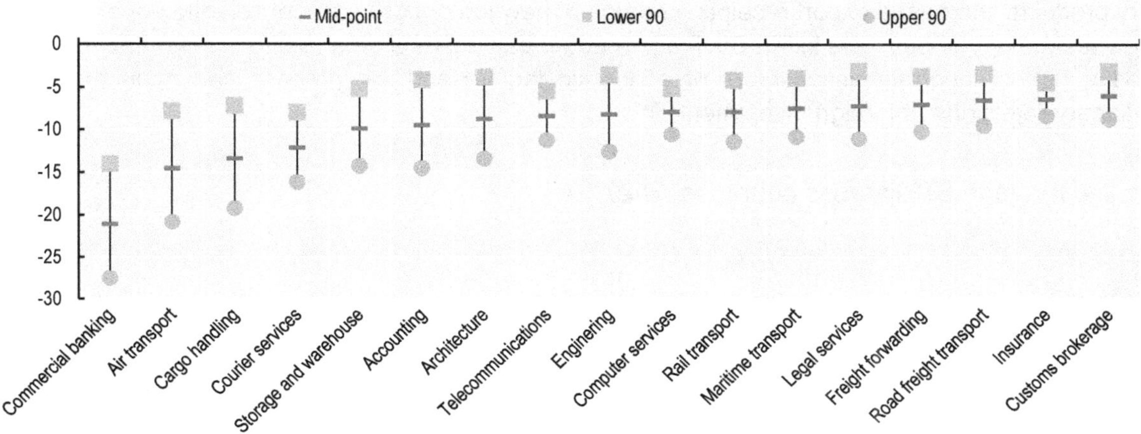

Note: Trade cost reduction in percentage of import value; 90% confidence intervals are computed using the standard errors of the trade elasticity estimated from a gravity model.
Source: OECD calculations using the STRI database and Benz and Jaax (2020[10]).

Trade costs due to strict regulations on services impact firms in all sectors, and smaller firms are more heavily impacted than larger firms. They are less likely to export or establish in less open markets than larger firms, and are less able to gain substantial market shares in challenging regulatory environments. Since women-owned and women-led businesses are generally smaller than those owned and led by men, they are more strongly impacted by the higher costs of services inputs into their production processes (see evidence above on women-led and women-owned businesses). The costs of complying with regulations – even more so with diverging regulations in every new market – fall more heavily on micro-, small- and medium-sized enterprises. For very small firms engaging in cross-border exports, an average level of services trade restrictiveness represents an additional 7% in trade costs relative to large firms. Establishing an affiliate abroad involves even higher costs: for a small firm, an average level of services trade restrictiveness is estimated to be equivalent to an additional 12% tariff compared to large firms (Rouzet, Benz and Spinelli, 2017[12]).

Horizontal services trade barriers

The 2020 STRI of New Zealand is slightly below the average of all countries in the STRI database, indicating that New Zealand's services-related regulations are slightly less restrictive that most other countries in the sample (Figure 2.4). This position is explained in large part by an overall favourable regulatory framework. Moreover, New Zealand's regulatory environment for services was relatively stable over the past years. However, some restrictions remain, representing unnecessary barriers to foreign services providers and hampering access of foreign services firms to the New Zealand market. At the same time, these barriers entail additional costs for domestic consumers and businesses relying on the services of foreign providers to facilitate their operations or their own exports. This section describes the horizontal barriers that apply in all services sectors.

Some restrictions remain related to the entry of foreign services providers. For example, the Companies Act requires that at least one member of a company's board of directors must be resident in New Zealand or Australia. This requirement may hamper the operations of small foreign-owned firms with incorporated subsidiaries in New Zealand. Moreover, the Overseas Investment Act requires that consent for investment in sensitive New Zealand assets, including business assets valued more than NZD 100 million. Such foreign investment is only approved when in New Zealand's national interest. The "Benefit to New Zealand test" includes economic factors, such as additional investment for development purposes, added market competition, greater efficiency or productivity or enhanced domestic services, increased processing of primary products, increased export receipts, creation of new job opportunities or retention of existing jobs, and new technology or business skills. Such a procedure can act as a deterrent to investment. In addition, there is a risk of incorrect assessment of economic factors and the process can open the door to discretionary rejections of foreign investment.

Figure 2.4. Average STRI across countries, 2020

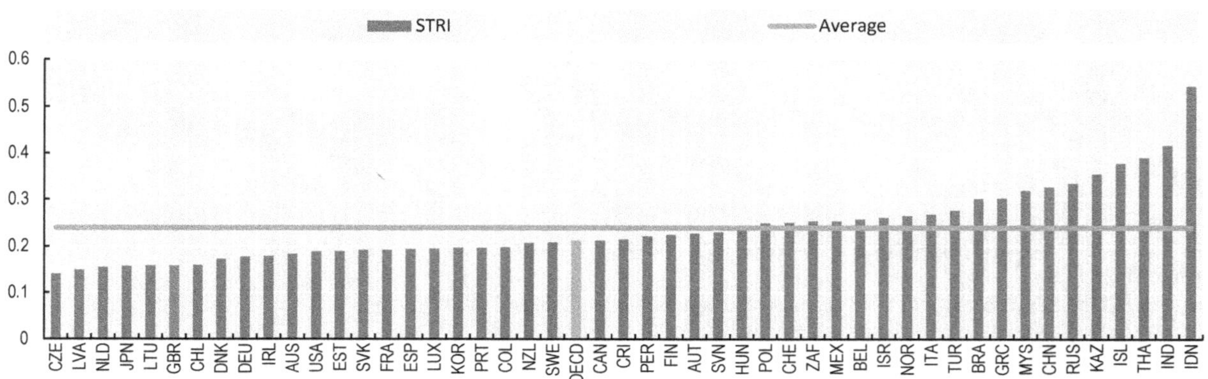

Note: The STRI indices take values between zero and one, one being the most restrictive. The STRI database records measures on a Most Favoured Nation basis. Air transport and road freight cover only commercial establishment (with accompanying movement of people). The indices are based on laws and regulations in force on 31 October 2020. The STRI regulatory database for the year 2020 covers the 38 OECD countries, Brazil, China, India, Indonesia, Kazakhstan, Malaysia, Peru, Russian Federation, South Africa, and Thailand.
Source: OECD (2020). STRI and TiVA databases.

Personal data can be transferred outside of New Zealand if it is subject to laws providing comparable safeguards to those in the New Zealand Privacy Act. At the same time, offshore storage of tax records according to the Tax Administration Act and the Goods and Services Tax Act is only possible under some conditions and on a case-by-case basis. Firms of all sizes and across all sectors use, process, and store data as part of their business models. While the protection of personal information is a legitimate policy objective, data regulation should be non-discriminatory and should not be more trade-restrictive than strictly necessary, achieving the dual goals of safeguarding data and enabling its flow across borders (Casalini, López González and Nemoto, 2021[13]).

Further horizontal restrictions exist in relation to the movement of natural persons. The initial duration of stay for contractual or independent services suppliers is twelve months on a Specific Purpose Visa. Intra-corporate transferees, however, are exempted from this restriction, facilitating stays in New Zealand of up to three years. New Zealand is not the only country offering visas with a relatively short duration of stay for temporary services providers. In fact, short duration of stays for contractual or independent services providers are relatively common across the OECD and other large economies covered in the STRI. Around half of all countries offer visas with an initial duration of stay of twelve months or less.

Moreover, this Specific Purpose Visa requires a labour market test, showing that it is not possible or appropriate for New Zealand citizens or residents to undertake an activity, however, a number of different regimes are grouped under this item, some of which are less restrictive than others. Such a requirement is relatively common, currently being applied in around three quarters of all countries in the sample. In order to ensure businesses have access to needed professionals, some countries apply a positive list of occupations for which employers are not required to show that workers are unavailable on the domestic labour market. In other countries, such a requirement can be waived if the foreign candidate's remuneration is above a certain threshold.

Scope for further horizontal liberalisation also results from a relatively long time and high cost for processing a business visa. While business visitors from a number of New Zealand's major trading partners benefit from visa waivers, lengthy and costly procedures can be a deterrent to Mode 4 (movement of natural persons) services trade with other countries. The processing time was around 28 days before the beginning of the COVID-19 pandemic and the fee for a business visitor visa was raised from NZD 170 to NZD 190 on 5 November 2018.[24] At the time of writing, visa processing for most applicants outside of New Zealand is still on hold due to travel restrictions implemented in the context of COVID-19.

New Zealand's regime on these two measures is more burdensome than the average and median of the OECD and other STRI countries. Median processing time for business visas is around 15 days while median cost of a business visa application is around USD 70. According to the STRI methodology, a processing time of less than ten days and a cost of less than USD 94 is required for a non-restrictive assessment of these measures.

New Zealand's services restrictiveness is below the average in 21 out of 22 sectors (Figure 2.5). The only exception is logistics cargo-handling. Other relatively restrictive sectors compared to the respective cross-country averages are logistics storage and warehousing, logistics freight-forwarding and computer services. The highest level of restrictiveness across sectors can be found for air transport services. However, this sector is subject to restrictive laws and regulations in a number of countries. For example, several countries apply foreign equity limitations in this sector, including New Zealand.

It should be noted that air transport connectivity, which is related to the level of restrictiveness in the sector, can have an enabling effect on trade in other services. The expansion of air travel has been found to account for 30% of total export growth in services on average (Benz and Jaax, 2022, forthcoming[14]). This suggests that services exporters rely on a set of complementary factors including in-person contact and business meetings. Air transport connectivity also positively impacts trade in goods. Countries with more frequent air connections trade more, and trade in more complex products. This is in part due to the share of goods trade that is transported by air (30% on average, half of which is transported in passenger planes) and the facilitating nature of business travel for increasing trade opportunities (Botero Garcia, Reshef and Umana-Dajud, 2021[15]).

Another enabling service, which has come to the foreground during the Covid-19 pandemic, is computer services and telecommunications connectivity. Moreover, it was seen above that women-led businesses tend to conduct much of their business online, in some cases more than men-led ones. Preliminary estimates imply that improvements in ICT infrastructure can explain roughly 30% of the total increase in services exports relative to domestic services consumption between 2000 and 2017 (Benz and Jaax, 2022, forthcoming[14]). New Zealand is less restrictive in these areas than the average of countries covered in the STRI, but is substantially more restrictive than the most liberal regimes (Figure 3.5).

By contrast, New Zealand's STRI is significantly lower than the cross-country average in legal services, accounting services, insurance and broadcasting. Insurance is also the sector with the lowest absolute STRI for New Zealand. In the insurance sector, New Zealand is relatively close to the least-restrictive country. In all other sectors, there is still significant scope for further liberalisation of services trade.

Figure 2.5. New Zealand STRI by sector, 2020

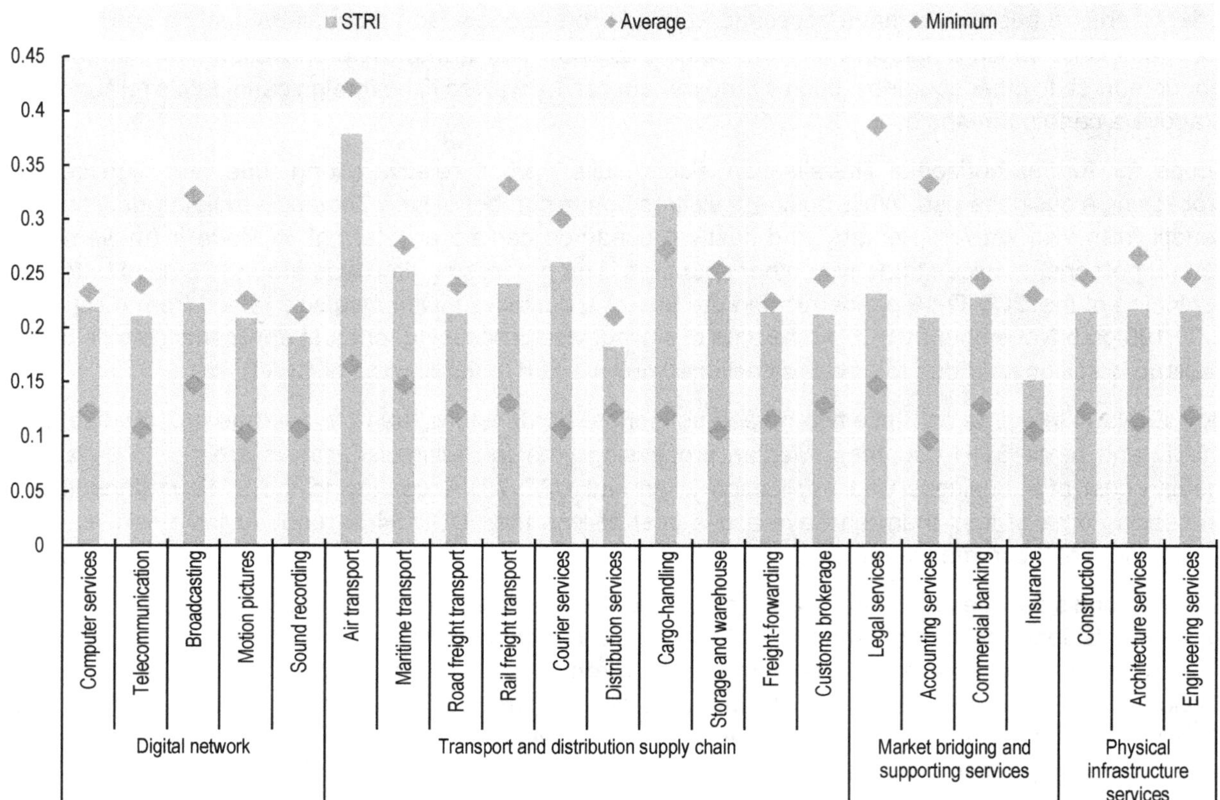

Note: The STRI indices take values between zero and one, one being the most restrictive. The STRI database records measures on a Most Favoured Nation basis. Preferential trade agreements are not taken into account. Air transport and road freight cover only commercial establishment (with accompanying movement of people). The indices are based on laws and regulations in force on 31 October 2020. The average is computed over the 48 countries covered by the STRI in 2020.
Source: STRI regulatory database.

A complementary feature in the STRI suite of tools is the Digital STRI. It measures cross-cutting barriers to digitally enabled services trade in all sectors and classifies barriers in five categories: infrastructure, electronic transactions, payments, weak intellectual property rights (trademark and copyright), and other barriers such as forced technology transfers (Ferencz, 2019[16]). New Zealand's restrictiveness towards digitally enabled services is below the average of countries covered. The majority of these barriers results from the category of infrastructure-related measures, similar to what is observed for other countries. Amongst others, this category includes restrictions to cross-border data flows, see above.

The following section digs deeper into the applicable laws and regulations in retail and wholesale distribution, a services sector where women are prevalent as workers and as business owners and leaders.

Trade restrictiveness in the distribution sector, where women are highly represented as workers and business owners and leaders

The retail trade sector is one of the main traded sectors in New Zealand where women are more likely to be employed than men, including in exporting firms.[25] The STRI for the distribution services sector covers general wholesale and retail sales of consumer goods (specific regulation of speciality distribution sectors such as pharmaceuticals and motor vehicles are not considered). The STRI in this sector also covers regulations relating to electronic commerce, given the increasing prevalence of multi-channel retail services as a form of distribution services.

New Zealand's restrictiveness for distribution services is very close to the average of all countries. Twenty-four countries were less restrictive and 23 countries were more restrictive than New Zealand in 2020. Other OECD countries with similar scores in this sector are France and Italy (Figure 2.6).

Figure 2.6. Trade restrictiveness in distribution services, 2020

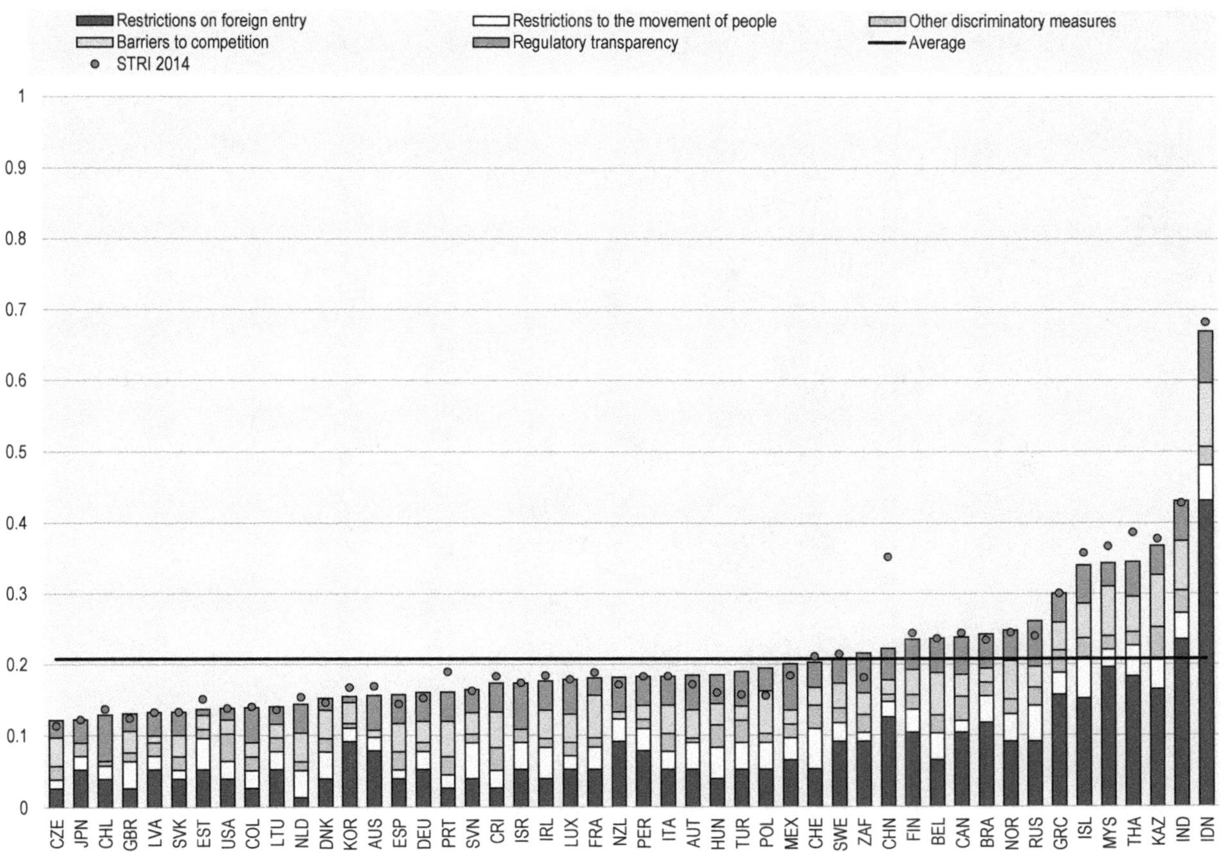

Note: The STRI indices take values between zero and one, one being the most restrictive. The STRI database records measures on a Most Favoured Nation basis. Air transport and road freight cover only commercial establishment (with accompanying movement of people). The indices are based on laws and regulations in force on 31 October 2020. The STRI regulatory database for the year 2020 covers the 38 OECD countries, Brazil, China, India, Indonesia, Kazakhstan, Malaysia, Peru, Russian Federation, South Africa, and Thailand.
Source: OECD (2020). STRI database.

This result might seem surprising when only comparing STRIs across sectors, such as in Figure 2.6. This figure shows that New Zealand's STRI in the distribution sector is the second lowest of all sectors. However, distribution is the sector with the least restrictions of all sectors (OECD, 2021[17]). Hence, in comparison with the international benchmark, New Zealand's performance looks slightly less impressive. Sector-specific restrictions mostly come from the regulatory transparency policy area and partly also related to barriers to competition.

When engaging with trading partners in negotiations of new or modernised trade agreements, negotiators could review New Zealand's and partner countries' levels of restrictiveness in services sectors where women engage most, such as distribution services and some professional services. These sectors could be prioritised for obtaining market access in partner countries, in particular if barriers to entry into those sectors are high. Trade negotiators could make use of the STRI sectoral database to ascertain which sectors are most highly restricted to trade.

In conclusion, less restrictive services sectors positively impact competitiveness of both services and goods sectors. Lower levels of services restrictiveness are strongly correlated with higher levels of services exports (Nordås and Rouzet, 2015[9]), where New Zealand women generally work and lead businesses. Overall, New Zealand's services sectors are generally more open than many of the other countries for which the OECD tracks services restrictions, although areas for consideration have been highlighted above.

References

Benz, S. and A. Jaax (2020), “The costs of regulatory barriers to trade in services: New estimates of ad valorem tariff equivalents”, *OECD Trade Policy Papers*, No. 238, OECD Publishing, Paris, https://doi.org/10.1787/bae97f98-en. [10]

Benz, S. and A. Jaax (2022, forthcoming), *Shedding light on drivers of services tradability over two decades*, OECD Publications, Paris. [14]

Botero Garcia, D., A. Reshef and C. Umana-Dajud (2021), “Moins d'avions, c'est mois de commerce”, *La lettre du CEPII*, Vol. December/422, http://www.cepii.fr/PDF_PUB/lettre/2021/let422.pdf. [15]

Casalini, F., J. López González and T. Nemoto (2021), “Mapping commonalities in regulatory approaches to cross-border data transfers”, *OECD Trade Policy Papers*, No. 248, OECD Publishing, Paris, https://doi.org/10.1787/ca9f974e-en. [13]

Ferencz, J. (2019), “The OECD Digital Services Trade Restrictiveness Index”, *OECD Trade Policy Papers*, No. 221, OECD Publishing, Paris, https://doi.org/10.1787/16ed2d78-en. [16]

Honey, S. (2018), *Will CPTPP Offer Tangible Improvements for Women?*, https://www.cigionline.org/articles/will-cptpp-offer-tangible-improvements-women/. [2]

Korinek, J., E. Moïsé and J. Tange (2021), “Trade and gender: A Framework of analysis”, *OECD Trade Policy Papers*, No. 246, OECD Publishing, Paris, https://doi.org/10.1787/6db59d80-en. [4]

López González, J. and S. Sorescu (2021), “Trade in the time of parcels”, *OECD Trade Policy Papers*, No. 249, OECD Publishing, Paris, https://doi.org/10.1787/0faac348-en. [7]

López González, J. and S. Sorescu (2019), “Helping SMEs internationalise through trade facilitation”, *OECD Trade Policy Papers*, No. 229, OECD Publishing, Paris, https://doi.org/10.1787/2050e6b0-en. [6]

Miroudot, S. and C. Cadestin (2017), “Services In Global Value Chains: From Inputs to Value-Creating Activities”, *OECD Trade Policy Papers*, No. 197, OECD Publishing, Paris, https://doi.org/10.1787/465f0d8b-en. [11]

Monteiro, J. (2018), “Gender related Provisions in Regional Trade Agreements”, *WTO Staff Working Paper ERSD-2018-15* December. [1]

Nordås, H. and D. Rouzet (2015), “The Impact of Services Trade Restrictiveness on Trade Flows: First Estimates”, *OECD Trade Policy Papers*, No. 178, OECD Publishing, Paris, https://doi.org/10.1787/5js6ds9b6kjb-en. [9]

OECD (2021), *The OECD Services Trade Restrictiveness Index: Policy Trends up to 2021*, https://www.oecd.org/trade/topics/services-trade/documents/oecd-stri-policy-trends-2021.pdf. [17]

OECD (2020), *OECD Services Trade Restrictiveness Index: Policy trends up to 2020*, https://www.oecd.org/trade/topics/services-trade/documents/oecd-stri-policy-trends-up-to-2020.pdf. [8]

OECD (2018), *Trade Facilitation and the Global Economy*, OECD Publishing, Paris, https://doi.org/10.1787/9789264277571-en. [5]

Rouzet, D., S. Benz and F. Spinelli (2017), "Trading firms and trading costs in services: Firm-level analysis", *OECD Trade Policy Papers*, No. 210, OECD Publishing, Paris, https://doi.org/10.1787/b1c1a0e9-en. [12]

World Trade Organization (2021), *Negotiations on Services Domestic Regulation Conclude Successfully in Geneva*, https://www.wto.org/english/news_e/news21_e/jssdr_02dec21_e.htm. [3]

Notes

[1] It is worth noting that even explicit gender-related provisions vary in their objectives. Some aim to promote gender equality, some refer to women's economic empowerment whilst some have the narrower objective of increasing women's participation in international trade. Other gender-related provisions seek to protect women (usually women workers) from adverse impacts of trade competition.

[2] See https://www.mfat.govt.nz/en/trade/free-trade-agreements/free-trade-agreements-under-negotiation/new-zealand-united-kingdom-free-trade-agreement/resources/agreement-in-principle.

[3] Article 19.10: Cooperation.

[4] Article 23.4: Women and Economic Growth.

[5] See Joint Declaration on Fostering Progressive and Inclusive Trade.

[6] See the Trade and Gender Chapters of the 2016 Chile–Uruguay trade agreement, the 2017 Canada–Chile, Argentina–Chile, Canada–Israel trade agreements, as well as the 2020 Brazil–Chile and Chile–Ecuador trade agreements.

[7] Table 201 presents New Zealand's trade agreements chronologically, showing that the inclusion of gender-related provisions is a recent development.

[8] Chapter 14.

[9] Chapter 24.

[10] Chapter 15.

[11] Chapter 15.

[12] Chapter 21.

[13] ILO Declaration on Fundamental Principles and Rights at Work.

[14] Article 19.5: Enforcement of Labour Laws.

[15] Article 19.7: Corporate Social Responsibility.

[16] CPTPP indicates that inclusive economic growth includes a more broad-based distribution of the benefits of economic growth (Article 23.1.2). Elsewhere, inclusive trade has been taken to refer to trade that all people, including vulnerable groups such as women, young people, Indigenous groups and small businesses, can contribute to and benefit from.

[17] NZ-Korea, Annex II, Services and Investment Non-Conforming Measures.

[18] The OECD Trade Facilitation Indicators cover the full spectrum of border procedures for more than 160 economies. The eleven indicators are: (a) information availability; (b) involvement of trade community; (c) advance rulings; (d) appeal procedures; (e)fees and charges; (f) formalities – documents; (g) formalities – automation; (h) formalities – procedures; (i) internal border agency co-operation; (j) external border

agency co-operation; (k) governance and impartiality. Detailed measures are available at: https://sim.oecd.org/default.ashx?ds=TFI .

[19] The analysis in this section is based on latest available from the 2019-20 Trade Facilitation Indicators (TFIs) database. The update for the 2021-22 TFIs database is ongoing until Q1 2022.

[20] World Bank Doing Business Trading Across Borders.

[21] The agencies included are: Customs, Ministry for Primary industries, Maritime NZ and Ministry of Health.

[22] OECD Digital Trade Inventory (2021): https://www.compareyourcountry.org/digital-trade-inventory-international-instruments; https://www.compareyourcountry.org/digital-trade-inventory-regional-trade-agreements .

[23] This analysis is based on the OECD Services Trade Restrictiveness Index (STRI). The STRI is an online regulatory database and composite index, collecting information on laws and regulations in 22 services sectors. As of 2021, the STRI regulatory database covers 50 economies, the 38 OECD countries, Brazil, China, India, Indonesia, Kazakhstan, Malaysia, Peru, Russian Federation, Singapore, South Africa, Thailand, and Viet Nam.

[24] The scoring in the OECD STRI is based on the regime faced by Indian nationals.

[25] Women work in many services sectors that are less traded such as health, education, child and elder care and personal services. None of those sectors are included in the STRI. This section covers one STRI sector where women tend to work, including in export-related jobs.

3. Forward policy actions for consideration

Chapter 3 suggests a number of policy actions that New Zealand could undertake to lower barriers to trade faced by women, to promote inclusive gains from trade, and to translate gender equality objectives into trade policies. These policy recommendations aim to contribute to New Zealand's inclusive trade agenda and support open markets and a rules-based international trading system in good working order.

Previous chapters have served to increase understanding about women's engagement in trade as workers, entrepreneurs and business leaders, and consumers, and the extent to which New Zealand's trade agreements reflect gender-specific concerns. In this section, a number of policy actions are suggested to lower barriers to trade faced by women, to increase their likelihood of reaping the benefits from trade, and to translate gender equality objectives into trade policies. These suggestions aim to contribute to the ongoing conversation on trade and gender in the context of New Zealand's Trade for All agenda.

The following trade and gender policy actions can help to ensure that open markets and a rules-based international trading system in good working order contribute to women's economic empowerment.

- Making trade agreements more gender-sensitive: *Ex ante* impact assessments, the optimisation of existing gender-related provisions, new or revised gender-responsive provisions, and strengthened monitoring and institutional support can make New Zealand's trade agreements more gender-sensitive.
- Support for gender-sensitive policymaking in plurilateral contexts: New Zealand could support and promote gender-responsive policy initiatives such as the Global Trade and Gender Arrangement (GTAGA), application of the non-discrimination clause in the WTO Reference Paper on Services Domestic Regulation, ongoing work in APEC and elsewhere on gender-responsive standards, and the ongoing initiatives in WTO on trade and gender.
- Communication of the benefits of trade agreements: SMEs are less aware and less able to take advantage of, the opportunities under trade agreements. Efforts to ensure that the benefits of trade deals are more widely understood, in particular by potential women exporters who may have more shallow networks, should be undertaken. Increasing public understanding of the benefits of trade and trade agreements more widely can also help to create constituencies that favour open markets
- Market access: New Zealand could prioritise market access reforms that would particularly benefit women. Although New Zealand is generally an open economy, there are areas, particularly as regards services, that could be considered for further market opening, including as regards movement of people. Lower income consumers, where women are disproportionately found, spend more of the income.
- Aid for Trade: Outside New Zealand, gender gaps are generally greater and women often face substantial legal and administrative barriers to their participation in economic activity in addition to strongly gendered cultural norms. Thus far, women's economic empowerment has not been a stated objective in New Zealand's Aid for Trade strategy. New Zealand could consider leveraging Aid for Trade to contribute to more gender equal outcomes by mainstreaming gender in its Aid for Trade strategy. The OECD and WTO are undertaking a comprehensive joint project on integrating gender equality objectives in Aid for Trade that could inform such a strategy.
- Trade facilitation: Women-owned and women-led businesses in New Zealand, as in other OECD countries, tend to be smaller than those led by men. Administrative processes that are costly, time consuming, and non-transparent increase trade costs of small firms more than large ones that have more resources to better navigate challenging business environments. Facilitating trade through simpler processes and more transparent procedures will increase small businesses' propensity to export, and decrease their trade costs. Although New Zealand ranks well among OECD countries in terms of facilitating trade, a more focused gender lens could be applied in order to ensure inclusivity in its policy formulation and those that are affected by facilitating measures.
- Representation of women: Ensuring that women are engaged in trade policymaking both as senior policy makers and as consulted stakeholders will go a long way to ensuring trade policies work for women. A first step requires monitoring their involvement at all levels of policymaking.
- Trade promotion: Export promotion has been prioritised in New Zealand, both in terms of resources devoted to it, and the services its trade promotion authority, NZTE, provides. These programmes

and services could be leveraged to ensure women entrepreneurs and exporters are fully supported in their export journeys.

- Professional and business networks: Women generally have shallower business networks (Korinek, Moïsé and Tange, 2021[1]) and seem to benefit less from traditional business networks (International Trade Centre, 2019[2]) than men. Although not strictly within the purview of government, some suggestions that aim to augment the usefulness of professional and business networks for women are included here.
- Data gaps: This Review combines different data sources and extracts as much gender-differentiated information as possible from existing sources. Increasing the collection of gender-differentiated data is one of the stated mandates both of the OECD 2021 Ministerial Council Statement[1] and the WTO Joint Ministerial Declaration on the Advancement of Gender Equality and Women's Economic Empowerment within Trade.[2]
- Domestic policies: Several domestic policy areas could be prioritised to ensure that women are in a position to take full advantage of the benefits of trade. Some of the major ones that have emerged from this Review of New Zealand are included here.

Making trade agreements more gender-sensitive

The New Zealand trade agreements that have been notified to WTO contain few gender-specific provisions. This section aims to indicate options for New Zealand to consider in future trade agreements to promote gender equality, women's economic empowerment, and women's participation in trade.

Ex ante impact assessments

Before entering into a trade agreement, New Zealand undertakes a comprehensive analysis of its impacts in the form of a National Interest Analysis (NIA). NIAs have increased greatly in scope and depth since they were first undertaken. They cover all chapters of the trade agreement and include computable general equilibrium (CGE) modelling of the impacts of greater market access and lowering of non-tariff measures. However, *ex ante* impact assessments do not presently include a gender dimension and do not generally include estimates of job gains and losses. Gender-differentiated assessments could be carried out as part of the NIA or as a stand-alone exercise,[3] and could be undertaken by New Zealand alone or through pooling resources with other Parties to the trade agreement under negotiation. In the case of an agreement with a less developed country, New Zealand could assess the potential for measuring the likely impacts on the partner country in a gender differentiated way or provide resources necessary for the partner country to carry out its own gender impact assessment.[4]

Assessments should measure gender-differentiated impacts of market access in at least the main sectors that the negotiations cover, identifying sectors in which new export markets could be of particular importance for New Zealand's women-led businesses or for women's employment. The scope of the NIAs could also include estimated price impacts of the trade agreement, which would shed further light on the agreement's impacts on more vulnerable groups and those in lower income categories where women are disproportionately represented. As trade agreements evolve to include more gender-specific provisions, NIAs could assess first-order effects – direct effects of changes in market access and trade reforms – but also indirect effects that will suggest how women may be impacted by the different chapters in the trade agreement.

Ex ante impact assessments can inform negotiating strategies. Trade negotiators could prioritise for new or increased market access and national treatment commitments those goods and, especially, services sectors that are of particular importance for New Zealand women workers or traders, as revealed by *ex ante* gender impact assessments and other studies such as this Trade and Gender Review. For example, efforts towards the mutual recognition of foreign qualifications in professional services could be strengthened, which could help to reduce entry barriers for foreign professionals but also open up overseas opportunities for New Zealanders. The OECD Services Trade Restrictiveness database can inform as to restrictions on services provision in New Zealand and in its partner countries. In some services where women are most present, e.g. education services, there is little trade. Specific modes of delivery of education services could be prioritised for trade, e.g. distance education (delivered through mode 1) and presence of natural persons (mode 4).

Impact assessments can also help to identify sectors in which women-led businesses or women's employment need to be supported in the face of foreign competition through scheduling of market access commitments within the trade agreement, or complementary policies or programmes.

Making the most of existing gender-related provisions

New Zealand's current trade agreements leave considerable room for introducing gender-responsive practices without amending the treaties, even in existing trade agreements that do not explicitly mention women, for example in provisions for cooperation and implementing arrangements.[5]

The list of cooperation areas that trade agreements or related Memoranda of Understanding (MoUs) identify are generally "not an exhaustive list and other items may be added to the cooperative programme."[6] Labour MoUs and chapters in several of New Zealand's existing trade agreements also provide for the participation of civil society in identifying areas for cooperation.[7]

Cooperation in the context of agreements with countries at a similar level of development or gender equality[8] could include: gathering and analysing data about gendered pay gaps within enterprises operating within each Party's territory;[9] sharing practices on parental leave, child care policies and formalisation of unpaid work; gathering and sharing gender-differentiated data on access to finance; sharing experience and information with a view to increasing women's participation on boards and in senior management roles; gender-positive policies as regards government procurement; supporting women and other vulnerable groups through trade promotion initiatives; and developing trade missions that are inclusive of women.[10] Cooperation in the context of agreements with countries at differing levels of gender equality and development could include, for example, capacity-building initiatives for women entrepreneurs including in the areas of agricultural extension, export readiness and digital skills.

New or revised gender-responsive provisions

New Zealand has a number of active negotiations under way that will include gender chapters or provisions, including the NZ-UK FTA, the NZ-EU FTA, and the Pacific Alliance FTA. These negotiations could give consideration to the recommendations below.

New Zealand could consistently signal its commitment to gender equality goals[11] and reaffirm recognised international legal standards on gender equality such as CEDAW, SDG5 and ILO Declaration or Conventions. References to legal standards could be phrased as "*Each Party reaffirms its commitment to implement its obligations under [relevant instrument]*" for trade agreements as between parties to these instruments (Box 3.1) or "*Parties undertake to consider ratifying or implementing [relevant instruments that it is not yet party to]*" in the case of a trade agreement with a country not yet party to an instrument that is important for gender equality, most notably CEDAW.

Box 3.1. Some examples of trade agreements referring to international gender equality legal frameworks

Modernized Canada-Israel Free Trade Agreement Gender Chapter Article 13.2: International Agreements

1. Each Party reaffirms its commitment to implement effectively the obligations under the Convention on the Elimination of all Forms of Discrimination Against Women, adopted by the United Nations General Assembly on 18 December 1979, and notes the general recommendations made under its Committee.
2. Each Party reaffirms its commitment to implement effectively its obligations under other international agreements addressing gender equality or women's rights to which it is party.

Modernized Canada-Chile Free Trade Agreement Appendix II - Chapter N bis-Trade and Gender

O1.2 The Parties recall Goal 5 of the Sustainable Development Goals in the United Nations 2030 Agenda for Sustainable Development, which is to achieve gender equality and empower all women and girls.

In agreements with countries where gender gaps are wide and included explicitly in legal and regulatory frameworks, cooperation provisions could include road maps that work toward making those national regulations and legal provisions more gender-equal. In agreements with countries that are more gender-equal, firms could be encouraged to share information on wages to improve knowledge about gender wage gaps and share best practices in reducing them.[12] This type of provision might be included in Services or Investment Chapters, "encouraging enterprises operating within a Party's territory or subject to its jurisdiction" to share wage information in the same way that recent trade agreements' investment chapters[13] encourage enterprises to voluntarily incorporate corporate social responsibility principles into their internal policies

New Zealand could continue to include non-regression clauses in future trade and investment agreements[14] with explicit reference to gender equality laws and policies.[15] Non-regression clauses could be included in the parts of future agreements that are subject to monitoring, review and dispute settlement mechanisms.

All Parties' right to regulate should be safeguarded. New Zealand practice includes protections for policy objectives such as public health, safety, environment, public morals, prudential financial reasons, and remedial action of historical discriminations against Māori. This has been done through definitions, exceptions and carve outs in its trade agreements. New Zealand goes much further than many other countries' in that it routinely includes a Treaty of Waitangi exception in its trade agreements. New Zealand could make explicit further policy priorities such as promotion of equality between women and men in its safeguards.

Provisions favourable to gender equality could be reaffirmed in case of conflict with a trade rule.[16] One way would be through adding reference to CEDAW and/or other legal frameworks in favour of gender equality in wording currently found in trade agreements' final provisions (new wording in italics): "Each Party reaffirms its rights and obligations under the WTO Agreement and other agreements to which the Parties are party, *including CEDAW*"[17] and subjecting the provision to dispute settlement.

Within the WTO, the Reference paper on services domestic regulation specifies that when "adopting or maintaining measures relating to the authorisation for the supply of a service, the Member shall ensure that [...] such measures do not discriminate between men and women." A footnote specifies that "Differential treatment that is reasonable and objective, and aims to achieve a legitimate purpose, and adoption by Members of temporary special measures aimed at accelerating de facto equality between men and women, shall not be considered discrimination for the purposes of this provision."[18] GTAGA includes similar wording. Future trade agreements could include provisions outlining how competent bodies work toward greater recognition of qualifications in services and mutual recognition of licenses.

Future negotiations could address issues of work permits for accompanying spouses of services providers. An asymmetry of behaviours by gender is often illustrated in willingness to leave employment opportunities to accompany a spouse who has been hired abroad: men may be less likely than women to interrupt their careers to follow their spouse's professional opportunity abroad. Moreover, dual earner couples have become the majority of couples in OECD countries, so regulations involving spouses' work status could be better mainstreamed. New Zealand could address the question of accompanying spouse visas in its bilateral trade negotiations, or as an issue for discussion in the plurilateral fora in which it participates.

Further review of SPS regulations and stronger disciplines on those that are overly burdensome and streamlining health-related border controls would benefit smaller producers and traders, including women, as would lower-income households where women are disproportionately found.

Monitoring and institutional support

The importance of monitoring and review of trade agreements provisions cannot be overstated. Agreements should set periodicity and dates for monitoring, indicate who is responsible for it, and specify that monitoring should include analysing differential impacts on men and on women using gender-disaggregated data. Gender-specific aspects to be monitored should include: whether women are availing themselves of the possibilities under the trade agreement, including indications of obstacles to women benefitting from the agreement and a description of the number, nature and impact on gender equality of the cooperation activities mandated by the agreement. It would be desirable to estimate the impacts on jobs of the trade agreements, using gender-differentiated data. Contact Points could be requested to provide gendered reporting on numbers of requests and notifications they receive as part of the monitoring mechanism. A provision could be considered specifying that summaries of the monitoring of the gendered aspects of the agreement should be submitted to the CEDAW Committee as part of the Parties' periodic reports to the Committee, and to the WTO as part of the Trade Policy Review process.

In the case that the monitoring exercise demonstrates that the agreement is accentuating inequalities between women and men (or for other vulnerable groups), the trade agreement should provide for remedial action to be taken.

The Trade and Gender Committee should be entrusted with a broad monitoring and review role with adequate funding ensured for the Committee's work, including for the monitoring and review mechanisms.

Future trade agreements should enable gender-related provisions to be subject to the dispute settlement mechanism provided in the agreement, such as in the Canada-Israel bilateral agreement.[19] In the case of agreements with countries at a very different level of gender equality to New Zealand, provisions that reaffirm countries' commitments to international labour standards such as ILO Conventions and CEDAW should be subject to dispute settlement if non-compliance is verified by those relevant bodies.

Support for gender-sensitive policymaking in plurilateral contexts

New Zealand could join with other like-minded countries to promote adherence to the Reference paper on services domestic regulation, the first WTO rule with a gender non-discrimination clause, among WTO Members and regional partners.[20] New Zealand could also continue to engage with regional partners to communicate on the benefits of GTAGA, and ensure the Arrangement is given high visibility. Regular meetings of regional bodies, or bilateral consultations on trade agreements with existing partners could be potential fora for such communications. New Zealand should continue its participation in the WTO Informal Working Group on Trade and Gender.

New Zealand could continue to support work on gender-responsive standards in regional and multilateral institutions such as APEC. This includes supporting inclusion of women in standard creation and standard compliance, namely by improving the gender balance of participants in the development of standards, ensuring that the content of standards is gender inclusive, and monitoring the implementation of standards to achieve gender balance. In APEC, New Zealand should continue to support the implementation of the La Serena Roadmap on Women and Inclusive Trade, and the ongoing work of the Policy Partnership on Women and the Economy to drive gender mainstreaming across APEC fora. Such work could potentially be brought subsequently to the WTO TBT Committee. New Zealand is also launching an APEC online gender analysis tool to help with building capability and mainstreaming gender analysis. This tool could be promoted for use in other fora.

Communication of the benefits of trade agreements

Discussions with women entrepreneurs suggest that there is a substantial disconnect between the opportunities negotiated by the New Zealand government and the understanding of how to take advantage of market access among MSMEs. In order for market access opportunities to be seized by small businesses, they need to understand what those opportunities are.[21] The second most important export challenge experienced by women entrepreneurs, after the distance from export markets, is navigating regulations in foreign markets.[22] This is particularly true in services sectors where the majority of women work and own businesses.[23] There is no best way to engage with the potential users of trade agreements. Some Ministries embark on road shows to discuss the benefits of recently-negotiated or modernised agreements; others engage with specific groups of stakeholders such as professional women's organisations or networks of MSMEs; others offer an online chat function to engage with interested exporters or potential exporters; some trade agreements such as the CPTPP include the provision of a 'one-stop shop' for SMEs to get information and better understand how the agreement could affect their businesses. New Zealand's trade promotion agency, New Zealand Trade and Enterprise (NZTE) could play a role as an interface between MFAT and women entrepreneurs or groups of small business owners and leaders. This is a considerable and well-known problem in many countries and could be prioritised; it would also increase public understanding of the benefits of trade and trade agreements more widely.

Market access

New Zealand is generally more open to trade than the OECD average, including in services sectors where women work most such as distribution services. Openness to trade in services, however, includes all four modes of services delivery. Moreover, it was seen above that a few traded goods that are specifically destined for women are subject to import tariffs.

Liberalisation of trade in services includes movement of people, which is regulated by different Ministries. The Special Purpose visa requires a labour market test where firms must document all the efforts they have made to hire New Zealand professionals. The long-term skills shortage list visa applies to a specific list of occupations. However, if an occupation is not included on the list, e.g. "programmer" is included but "games designer" is not, requests are generally rejected. Both processes have been reported by entrepreneurs to be lengthy as requests are reviewed by various administrations including immigration, the qualifications authority (NZQA) and NZTE. Ensuring a wider definition of those covered by visa categories and included on skills shortage lists, streamlining of procedures, and enhanced coordination among administrations could reduce delays and allow entrepreneurs to access needed talent. In some countries, for example, skills requirements are waived if the foreign candidate's remuneration is above a certain threshold, indicating that they possess specific skills that are difficult to source. Although the challenge of accessing visas is not specific to women entrepreneurs, one or few unfilled positions can have a large impact in their smaller businesses.[24] Moreover, they often work in sectors that are less traditional, so occupations may be emerging and less well covered on lists of skills shortages.

Although they comprise a small part of household budgets, period products (tampons, sanitary napkins) come at a cost borne solely by women and girls. The tariff revenue collected on period products in 2019 was NZD 100 000 (see chapter on women consumers above). It is likely that this import tariff, although small and often waived, will be passed onto consumers. Given New Zealand's progressive stance on period poverty,[25] making period products available to girls in schools for free, it seems incoherent to charge for importing such products at the border. New Zealand could consider making imports of period products tariff free.

Aid for Trade

New Zealand's development assistance budget in 2020 was about NZD 820 million (MFAT, 2021[3]). About 25% of New Zealand's aid can be attributed to Aid for Trade.[26] In 2020-21, gender equality was a priority for scaling up its Overseas Development Assistance (ODA),[27] with the aim of having 60% of ODA including gender equality as a significant objective for undertaking development assistance activities. Mainstreaming gender equality in the Aid for Trade component of ODA could be a specific priority, potentially targeting a share of the budget to activities destined to increase women's participation in trade in recipient countries. Given New Zealand's global comparative advantages, its Aid for Trade funds could specifically target women in agriculture with better access to finance, facilitating access to agricultural inputs and technologies, compliance with SPS and TBT regulations and agricultural extension;[28] or implement programmes connecting women in lower-income countries to markets through access to digital technologies and use of digital platforms.

Work is underway in OECD and WTO to carry out an analysis that aims to shed light on how aid for trade can better impact gender equality, and provide concrete technical support, methods and indicators for governments to better integrate gender issues in their aid for trade strategies. The main areas of focus of aid for trade projects with a gender lens include: capacity building and technical assistance; economic and trade infrastructure; access to credit and equity; networking and digital platforms; and trade and investment climate. A first step may be to evaluate what types of programmes are already underway or recently completed in the Pacific region, where New Zealand engages most of its development assistance. The Development Assistance Committee of the OECD collects data on development assistance programmes with a gender focus and classifies those that are trade-related. In the first instance, the project underway in OECD will highlight some successful aid for trade initiatives that have a gender focus, including in the Pacific region. OECD and WTO could examine the specific case of New Zealand's aid for trade strategy in the context of their joint project.

Trade facilitation

As highlighted above, New Zealand ranks well in its trade facilitation performance as compared with other OECD countries and worldwide best practice. Moreover, smaller sized businesses particularly from streamlined and transparent border processes, in particular women-led businesses which tend to be smaller. Some selected areas could nevertheless be further strengthened. More particularly, its trade facilitation processes could be made more gender sensitive by ensuring the participation of women in its consultations and in its exporter programmes, and further adapting its working methods to SMEs.

Areas where further efforts could strengthen its performance and support women-led businesses both as exporters and importers are simplification of documents and streamlining of procedures, including through digital tools. These can provide women-led businesses and SMEs with increased predictability of cross-border trade transactions undertaken.

Few MSMEs in New Zealand appear to be currently in the AEO programme *Secure Exports Scheme*. In addition, the current registration system does not capture gender-related characteristics of the companies covered by the programme. In order to design strategies that could help increase the coverage of MSMEs and women-led businesses in the AEO programme, more information needs to be collected on the challenges encountered by such firms in meeting requirements to become an AEO and going through the certification process. Targeted outreach to MSMEs and women-led businesses would help firms address these challenges. In addition, explicit strategies could be implemented among border agencies to harmonise the requirements for AEOs, coordinate the certification, manage the follow-up, and coordinate the inspection of AEOs.

More generally, data content and structure and interoperability aspects are by far the most challenging in terms of improving the operation of the Trade Single Window (TSW). Further improvements could build on the progress made in terms of cross-border risk management co-operation, and could focus on aligning data requirements with trading partners' Single Windows and legal frameworks allowing for the sharing of submitted data.[29]

In the area of transparency, the average time between publication and entry into force of trade-related regulations could be increased to allow traders, including women-led businesses, more time to adjust their operations. Customs could also consider publishing on its website more comprehensive information on decisions and examples of Customs classification and judicial decisions relating to appeal procedures in order to help guide businesses.[30]

Additional and user-friendly information could be made available on specific processes trade agreements cover on small parcels (e.g. *de minimis,*[31] specific customs declaration or clearance procedures). Beyond existing trade agreements, more information on taxes and border procedures applied in other markets when exporting small parcels, as well as on how to import small parcels to New Zealand, could be centralised and provided on the Customs website. This can be valuable for many small, women-led businesses, who often engage in parcel trade. In addition, outreach on how to exploit new internationalisation opportunities through trade in parcels could be considered in the context of partnerships such as GTAGA. New Zealand could suggest in the context of GTAGA experience-sharing dialogues and joint implementation of co-operation activities (e.g. on border procedures, including for small parcels, use of Single Windows) to facilitate women's access to international trade opportunities.

More information could also be made available to guide small businesses - including those that are women-led - on advance rulings systems in economies beyond those with which New Zealand has trade agreements, which could help them access competitively-priced inputs as well as reduce fixed costs of accessing new markets.[32]

The private sector is currently not a member of New Zealand's National Committee on Trade Facilitation (NCTF).[33] Increasing involvement of associations representing women-led businesses and MSMEs through the NCTF or other structures for regular consultations with the private sector can help identify any inefficiencies and coordination challenges faced in the interaction with Customs or other border agencies when trading (including when using enquiry points, as well as challenges at specific border posts,[34] for specific sectors or when trading with specific countries).

Moreover, New Zealand already organises outreach programmes prior to the implementation of international agreements, including agreements that facilitate trade, where women-led businesses are extensively involved. This could provide a basis for outreach, engagement and targeted campaigns on additional topics that can facilitate trade. Such actions can also be supported by the recently established Trade Policy, Engagement and Implementation division in MFAT.

Finally, additional legal challenges will need to be addressed in the digitalisation of trade processes. The OECD Digital Trade Inventory (DTI) highlights that New Zealand has not yet ratified the UN Convention on the Use of Electronic Communications in International Contracts nor the 2017 UNCITRAL Model Law on Electronic Transferable Records (MLETR), which aims to enable the legal use of electronic transferable records both domestically and across borders. The availability of transferable documents and instruments in electronic form benefits digital trade, allowing for faster and more secure transmission while reducing risks associated with unauthorised duplication (Nemoto and López González, 2021[4]).

Representation of women

New Zealand should be commended for its public consultations, both in the context of NIAs and its diverse Trade for All Advisory Board. However, women currently appear under-represented in the submissions to consultations on New Zealand's planned trade agreements: the vast majority come from business groups in industries which tend to be male-dominated, especially in the primary sectors where many of the submissions originate. Deliberately involving women and women's groups in the consultation and assessment processes could include engaging and seeking input from sector-specific women's professional organisations and other civil society partners and stakeholder groups. Such sector-specific organisations for women exist in some of the larger export sectors such as meat and dairy.

Greater efforts could be made to ensure that women are represented in trade negotiating teams and in trade bodies, and encourage diversity in trade negotiating teams in partner countries. Whilst New Zealand currently has women in a range of senior trade positions,[35] the gender balance could be better monitored over time and consideration could be given to formalising a gender balance objective in trade-related positions. Moreover, striving to redress the gender balance amongst trade arbitrators could be done through stipulating that at least one arbitrator in any case be a woman, or through a more general provision such as that "Parties shall take active steps to increase the gender balance amongst arbitrators."

Trade promotion

New Zealand has prioritised trade promotion and has a strong presence among export promotion agencies globally. New Zealand Trade and Enterprise (NZTE), New Zealand's trade promotion agency, supports exporters with a wide range of services in New Zealand and in all major export markets. It has recently broadened its scope to support 1400 firms with a range of services, up from 700 previously. Sixteen per cent of the contact points for firms are women;[36] this is a similar share as previously when fewer firms were engaged. In order to enhance New Zealand's substantial support to its exporters and increase participation of women in the activities of NZTE, the following suggestions could be considered.

- NZTE could further reach out to women's professional networks and networks of small business owners and leaders to ensure the offer of services is known, and procedures for accessing export promotion assistance are understood. NZTE could increase its knowledge base of engagement with women entrepreneurs by collecting information on the number of women contacts or women-led firms that make contact with the agency, the share that become customers and the level of services offered to them.
- Gender-specific targets could be considered for inclusion of women-owned and women-led businesses in the 1400 Focus firms. Such targets could be progressively augmented. Targets could also be set for other less-represented groups. Beyond targets, encouraging an intentional approach toward women entrepreneurs and exporters may be required. NZTE customer managers have a certain amount of discretion in supporting clients and could be sensitised to the fact that potential women clients that may have less access to information regarding NZTE services due to their shallower networks and may therefore be less precise and demanding in their requests for

services. When 'pitching' a firm to an independent panel that decides whether firms become 'Focus' firms with access to more NZTE services and resources, characteristics such as the gender of the manager could be omitted. Alternatively, a different set of criteria for inclusion in Focus firms could be considered for women as for other target groups.

- New Zealand should be commended for prioritising export promotion[37] and for including in its export promotion priorities support for women entrepreneurs, illustrated not least of all by the recent nomination of a specialised Women in Export Lead in NZTE. This prioritisation should facilitate the development of the NZTE network of women exporters, and work toward ensuring the support they receive is tailored to their needs. Consideration could be given to making the Women in Export Lead a permanent position to ensure support builds over time.
- Ensure the new and fast-growing sectors of export activity such as digital services,[38] creative industries and services more generally – where women are highly represented – are well represented among NZTE Focus firms[39] and well supported among NZTE experts. Consider expanding the sector-specific events organised by NZTE in these sectors.
- Ensure that NZTE services in new markets, and markets that may be less welcoming to women entrepreneurs, such as the Middle East and parts of Asia, are intentional in their support of women entrepreneurs and business leaders. NZTE could also develop a programme to connect New Zealand women exporting to the Middle East, for example, with women business leaders present in the overseas market (such as a KEA network).
- Ensure that women are represented in New Zealand's trade missions and conferences. A first step would be to develop a more deliberate approach to the membership of trade missions, including developing a strategy to better represent women and other under-represented groups. Such an approach should require collection of gender-differentiated information on participation in trade delegations. Representation on trade missions often targets CEOs but women are often better represented at the "CEO minus 1" or other levels of leadership. Promoting a move toward greater gender balance in trade missions would also serve to present a more diverse reflection of New Zealand businesses. Ensuring that women are represented in trade conferences, many of which receive government agency support, also gives women exporters more visibility and valuable experience.
- Collecting gender-differentiated data on NZTE investment initiatives, in order to track the amount of investment going to women-led firms is also important. Where investment in women-led firms is lacking, a closer examination of the ecosystem of women-led firms could be undertaken, to better understand how to match entrepreneurs and investor, and pitch firms.

Professional and business networks

A well-documented challenge for women entrepreneurs and women business leaders is that they have shallower business networks (Korinek, Moïsé and Tange, 2021[1]).[40] Women report that they get less from traditional, male-dominated professional and business networks (International Trade Centre, 2019[2]). This means they have less access to information, fewer contacts and less mentoring and support than men. Many women's professional networks exist in New Zealand but it is not immediately clear which add value and whom they target. A mapping of professional networking organisations and their objectives and characteristics could be undertaken to increase understanding of the landscape of these organisations. Such a mapping could also inform further engagement with relevant organisations in the context of consultations on trade reforms or trade agreements.

Some women's professional organisations seem rather segmented, e.g. including only women business leaders of large firms; some exclude potential members through high annual fees or invitation-only requirements. Although these organisations may justifiably target a specific population of women business leaders, they could be encouraged to institute mentoring programmes for younger or early-stage entrepreneurs, or include a small number of 'scholarship' members for whom fees are lowered or waived. Since women business leaders in top positions have particularly high demands on their time, a one-to-many mentoring system could be suggested in some cases.

NZTE has started developing a network of women exporters that are contact points in NZTE client firms. This network could be expanded, providing training in areas where women entrepreneurs feel they need support;[41] organising information sessions on procedures necessary for different aspects of importing and exporting; engaging with officials on the content and implications of specific trade agreements; and showcasing successful women entrepreneurs and their journey to export.[42] One area where women could be better supported is with financial and credit advice; it was seen above that women seek financial advice less often than men. Networking events among women entrepreneurs could also be envisaged by NZTE, around sector-specific exporting, or new exporters, or specific export markets.[43]

Filling data gaps

This *Review* has pointed to a number of data gaps. Services and digital trade data was not available to combine with firm-level data to give a complete picture of women-owned and women-led businesses in the services sectors, where women are concentrated. While firm-level data on gender and other distributional characteristics is available in the LBD/IDI, it could be made more widely accessible via official published statistics.

There is a lack of recent data on unpaid labour within the household: the latest time-use survey was conducted in 2009-10. A new time-use survey is needed to better understand the time spent in unpaid labour that holds women back from contributing in the workplace, driving their businesses and networking.

Consumption data by household composition, including by gender, would give a clearer picture of the impact of trade on prices for women consumers. Better understanding consumption patterns of women-led single parent households or older women would shed further light on the impacts of trade on more vulnerable households.

A number of areas where gender-differentiated data could be collected have been outlined above, such as the participation of women in trade delegations, firm-level gender pay gaps and the extent to which women entrepreneurs are engaged in trade facilitating programmes. Other areas exist, such as gender-differentiated credit scores, and comprehensive data on requests for credit and share of loans allocated.

This *Review* has pointed to a number of areas where data had not previously been exploited to shed light on women in trade and the barriers they face. Applying a gender lens to new or updated data sources, and exploring how to combine data in innovative ways should be continued, in order to inform further on trade's impacts on women. There could be benefit in establishing a cross-agency data group to progressively address data issues.

Domestic policy priorities

Although New Zealand ranks fourth globally on gender equality – outranked only by Iceland, Finland and Norway – it ranks somewhat lower (66th globally) in gender income disparity (WEF, 2020). This may be due to many women working part-time in order to perform unpaid tasks, to the gender wage gap, and to the difficulty of women in all countries including New Zealand to access the highest levels of business and public service. These areas could be prioritised in order to ensure the New Zealand women can fully participate in the labour market and in trade.

Policies that move some of women's unpaid labour into the paid labour market will support working women. This is especially true for household chores, tasks that individuals often choose to engage in less compared with, for example, caring for children. Some New Zealand entrepreneurs have suggested allowing childcare to be considered a business expense, or reinstating a previous rebate for childcare costs. Other countries' responses to transferring unpaid work into the paid workforce have been varied. In France, for example, the *chèque emploi service* allows families and individuals to partially deduct household and childcare expenses from their federal income taxes. Research has shown that one of the main determinants of women's participation in the labour force is accessible and affordable childcare (OECD, 2017[5]).

Although gender wage gaps in New Zealand are substantially lower (9%) than the OECD average (13%), steps could be taken to close them further. Many OECD countries have instituted some form of pay transparency or related measures.[44] Some countries have instituted reforms aimed at greater pay transparency; in France, for example, medium-sized and large firms, as well as the public sector, must disclose salaries and employment by gender. In Switzerland, firms are obliged to comply with gender pay gap reporting requirements and must be certified that they are making sufficient progress toward parity in order to be eligible for government procurement contracts.

Ensuring women access the highest level of firm governance is a challenge in every country. Some of the higher performing countries such as Iceland and France have implemented quotas, generally of around 40%, for women's participation on boards. Some stock exchanges, including the New Zealand Stock Exchange (NZX), have insisted on greater disclosure of the gender composition of top management and board members. The Nasdaq, for example, has required disclosure of the gender composition of the management of its listed firms. The NZX requires listed companies to report on the gender breakdown of the directors and officers for each financial year.

Government procurement targets can be a powerful tool[45] to encourage economic activity by more vulnerable groups,[46] including within the trade policy toolbox. New Zealand could begin by collecting information on the share of government procurement contracts (at the national level, or also including local governments) that are filled by women-owned or women-led businesses, as has been started for Māori businesses.

References

BERL (2022), *New Zealand Women in Export Trade: Understanding the barriers*, Schulze, H.; Yadav, U.; Riley, H.; Dixon, H. (Draft mimeo). [6]

FAO (2011), *The State of Food and Agriculture, Women in Agriculture – Closing the gender gap for development*, http://www.fao.org/3/i2050e.pdf. [11]

International Trade Centre (2019), *From Europe to the World: Understanding Challenges for European Businesswomen, Sept. 30*, https://www.intracen.org/uploadedFiles/intracenorg/Content/Publications/From%20Europe%20to%20World%20Women%20EU_final_web.pdf,. [2]

Korinek, J., E. Moïsé and J. Tange (2021), "Trade and gender: A Framework of analysis", *OECD Trade Policy Papers*, No. 246, OECD Publishing, Paris, https://doi.org/10.1787/6db59d80-en. [1]

López González, J. and S. Sorescu (2021), "Trade in the time of parcels", *OECD Trade Policy Papers*, No. 249, OECD Publishing, Paris, https://doi.org/10.1787/0faac348-en. [8]

MFAT (2021), *New Zealand International Development Cooperation 2020-21*, http://, https://www.mfat.govt.nz/assets/Aid-Prog-docs/Policy/New-Zealands-International-Development-Cooperation-2020-21.pdf. [3]

Nemoto, T. and J. López González (2021), "Digital trade inventory: Rules, standards and principles", *OECD Trade Policy Papers*, No. 251, OECD Publishing, Paris, https://doi.org/10.1787/9a9821e0-en. [4]

NZTE (2020), *Annual Report 2019/20*, https://www.nzte.govt.nz/page/government-publications-media. [7]

OECD (2021), *Pay Transparency Tools to Close the Gender Wage Gap*, OECD Publishing, Paris, https://doi.org/10.1787/eba5b91d-en. [9]

OECD (2019), *Trade Policy Brief: Engaging and consulting on trade agreements*, https://issuu.com/oecd.publishing/docs/engaging_and_consulting_on_trade_agreements. [10]

OECD (2017), *Dare to Share: Germany's Experience Promoting Equal Partnership in Families*, OECD Publishing, Paris, https://doi.org/10.1787/9789264259157-en. [5]

Rimmer, S. (2017), *Gender-smart Procurement: Policies for Driving Change*, https://www.chathamhouse.org/2017/12/gender-smart-procurement-policies-driving-change. [12]

Notes

[1] "We call upon the OECD to model best practices in gender mainstreaming throughout its work, including through disaggregated data collection and analysis" (OECD 2021 Ministerial Council Statement, https://www.oecd.org/mcm/MCM-2021-Part-2-Final-Statement.EN.pdf, 5-6 October).

[2] The first of four objectives of the Joint Declaration is to: "Continue to review, develop and improve national and/or regional collection of gender-disaggregated data that is comparable to the extent possible and analysis on trade and gender, to provide the basis for informed gender-responsive policies" (WTO/MIN(21)/4/Rev.1).

[3] These could be based on existing methodologies, e.g. Government of Canada (2020), UNCTAD (2017).

[4] Consistent with New Zealand's development cooperation, e.g. (MFAT, 2021[3]).

[5] For example, the Technical Barriers to Trade (TBT) Chapters of recent FTAs include a provision that allows the Parties to develop implementing arrangements setting out new areas of cooperation with a view to removing regulatory barriers to the movement of goods, and facilitating trade, between the Parties or details for the implementing of the chapter. Such mechanisms allow the chapter to stay relevant and fit-for-purpose in addressing current and future TBT issues and opportunities.

[6] See e.g. NZ-China Free Trade Agreement National Interest Analysis; Memorandum of Agreement (MoA) on Labour Cooperation between the Government of New Zealand and the Government of the Republic of the Philippines, Article 3.

[7] See, for example, NZ-China; NZ-Philippines Labour MoA; CPTPP.

[8] As reflected in, for example, their ranking in the WEF Global Gender Gap Report; composite indicators of the World Bank's Women, Business and the Law dataset; or information included in SheTrades Outlook.

[9] Of New Zealand's trade agreements with labour provisions or side-agreements, CPTPP comes closest to naming this possibility under its cooperation provisions in the Labour Chapter; other agreements leave room for this type of activity.

[10] Extensive areas of cooperation can be found in GTAGA and in the Canada-Israel bilateral trade agreement.

[11] Possible wording: *"The Parties recognize gender equality as an important public policy objective. The Parties seek to ensure that the implementation of this agreement provides equal opportunities for women and men to participate in trade, and that its implementation does not inadvertently undermine national gender equality and women's rights commitments"* (adapted from ITC (2020) and ITC (2021)).

[12] In line with emerging legislative practice in countries such as Austria, Iceland, France, Switzerland and the United Kingdom, who have pay transparency laws.

[13] See, for example, CPTPP Investment Chapter Article 9.17: Corporate Social Responsibility; USCMA Investment Chapter Article 14.17: Corporate Social Responsibility.

[14] Several of New Zealand's trade agreements specify that it is inappropriate to lower the levels of protection afforded by domestic environmental, labour or human rights laws in order to encourage trade and investment.

[15] This wording is common in other countries' trade and investment agreements. See, for example, Canada's PTAs with Peru 2009 and Colombia 2011.

[16] This would also respond to concerns expressed by New Zealanders in the Trade for All process, that conflicts between trade rules and other international agreements are addressed within a trade law framework leading to favouring trade rules where there is conflict between trade and other rules. See Trade for All Report (2019).

[17] AANZFTA Final Provisions: Article 2 Relation to Other Agreements.

[18] WTO (2021) Reference Paper on Services Domestic Regulation, Note by the Chairperson, INF/SDR/1, 27 September 2021.

[19] Article 13.6 of Canada-Israel provides a dispute settlement mechanism for gender provisions with binding but not compulsory jurisdiction.

[20] Sixty-seven countries, including New Zealand, endorsed the Joint Initiative at the conclusion of the negotiations on 2 December 2021.

[21] This challenge is not specific to New Zealand: "SMEs can be less aware of the opportunities under trade agreements, or much less able to take advantage of them" (OECD, 2019[10]).

[22] According to the OECD-World Bank-Facebook survey. See section on women entrepreneurs and business leaders.

[23] Many women business leaders "did not have a complete understanding of what FTAs were or how they could play a role in their decision making" according to a study of women entrepreneurs in New Zealand (BERL, 2022[6]).

[24] Discussions with women entrepreneurs, particularly those engaged in new and growing sectors, have elucidated difficulties they have experienced in hiring foreign professionals. This is particularly acute in the digital technology sectors. Some firms have offshored their development operations because they cannot obtain visas for potential hires. In this case, both jobs and the income tax of the job holders are relinquished from New Zealand.

[25] See https://www.education.govt.nz/our-work/overall-strategies-and-policies/wellbeing-in-education/access-to-free-period-products/

[26] Aid for Trade at a Glance, https://public.tableau.com/views/Aid_for_trade/Aid_for_trade?:embed=y&:showTabs=y&:display_count=no&:showVizHome=no#1, accessed 13 December 2021.

[27] See https://www.mfat.govt.nz/assets/Peace-Rights-and-Security/International-security/Gender-Action-Plan-2021-2025.pdf

[28] While woman make up on the average close to half of the agricultural labour force in developing countries, 5% of all agricultural extension services are directed towards women and 15% of the world's extension agents are woman (FAO, 2011[11]). Moreover, the Green Box (i.e. Annex 2 of the WTO Agreement on Agriculture) allows for unlimited support through measures that can target women such as training, research, extension and advisory services.

[29] An assessment is ongoing on enhancing interoperability with the ASEAN Single Window, which can provide important guidance for further facilitating trade between New Zealand and ASEAN member economies.

[30] More information could also be made available to guide small businesses – including those that are women-led – on how to best make use of the advance rulings system when importing specific inputs. In the context of trade agreements, information on using advance rulings systems across different trading partners can also help businesses reduce fixed costs of accessing new markets.

[31] *De minimis* concerns thresholds below which either import duties and/or VAT do not apply or for which customs procedures, including data requirements, are simplified (López González and Sorescu, 2021[8]).

[32] Advance rulings can reduce disputes at the actual moment of release or clearance with the Customs authority on tariff headings, valuation and origin (i.e. eligibility to preferential treatment) and consequently delays are avoided.

[33] The NCTF is located within the Trade Policy and Negotiations Division (TPND) of the New Zealand Ministry of Foreign Affairs and Trade (MFAT). It draws in officials from other parts of MFAT, including the Pacific and Development Group, and the New Zealand Customs Service, Ministry for Primary Industries, Ministry of Business, Innovation and Employment and New Zealand Trade and Enterprise as required.

[34] Specific contact points at selected border posts could be considered.

[35] For example, as of early 2022, New Zealand's Permanent Representative and Deputy Permanent Representative to the WTO and the OECD are all women, as are several Chief Negotiators and the Special Agricultural Trade Envoy.

[36] This is an unofficial estimate. NZTE could monitor the participation of women-led and women-owned businesses among its customer base. A definition of women-owned and women-led businesses agreed by multiple international organisations and standards bodies can be found here: https://www.sis.se/en/about_sis/isoiwa-34-definition-of-a-womanowned-business-and-guidance-on-its-use/.

[37] NZTE has a budget of NZD 250 million (about EUR 150 million) and 750 staff, 68% of which are customer-facing (NZTE (2020[7]) and https://www.nzte.govt.nz/page/about-nzte).

[38] Interviews of New Zealand women business leaders conducted by BERL confirmed their interest in having "a bigger and more specialised team" in the "emerging and valuable" technology sector (BERL, 2022[6]).

[39] In 2019-20, the last year for which data are publicly available, NZTE Focus firms included 25% of tech firms and 10% of other services firms and. The remaining 65% were in manufacturing and food and beverage sectors.

[40] In a set of interview with New Zealand business leaders, many indicated that they "did not have any common networks with exporters in their industry. However, majority of them pointed out that they would like to have the opportunity to build connections and share knowledge and other resources with like-minded local business owners." However, the small number of women that did develop such networks with other exporters in their industries "shared knowledge about markets and experiences with one another. In some cases they also shared shipping containers to save costs" (BERL, 2022[6]).

[41] Women entrepreneurs indicate more frequently than men that they consider they have inadequate skills to run their businesses (Korinek, Moïsé and Tange, 2021[1]). Although women who run a business have

higher levels of educational attainments than men, they tend to have less experience in self-employment and continue to have fewer opportunities than men in management positions, which acts as a barrier to gaining management experience and skills that are useful for entrepreneurship (OECD, 2019a). Skills that women entrepreneurs indicate they lack in New Zealand include business strategy, cash flow management, and scaling a business and a team.

[42] Showcasing successful women entrepreneurs is an important step toward changing mindsets regarding what an exporter looks like. On the NZTE website, for example, a set of 14 inspiring videos present New Zealand exporters, their passions and their export journeys. Two are women-led and one is led by both a woman and a man (equalling a gender balance of 80% men and 20% women).

[43] A similar recommendation emerged from a set of interviews of women business leaders in a separate qualitative process (BERL, 2022[6]).

[44] Eighteen of the 38 OECD countries mandate systematic, regular gender wage gap reporting by private sector firms. Within this group, nine implemented comprehensive equal pay auditing processes, which require additional gender data analysis and typically propose follow-up strategies to address inequalities. Just under half of OECD countries use job classification systems, which attempt to standardise pay and make it transparent by gender and within specific job categories (OECD, 2021[9]).

[45] Before the COVID-19 pandemic, spending on government procurement in New Zealand represented about 20% of its GDP.

[46] The United States, for example, has a procurement target of 5% of the value of federal contracts going to women-led businesses; Canada targets indigenous communities in its outreach and prioritisation of procurement. Switzerland awards government procurement contracts only to firms that have certified gender wage transparency. The United States target was met for the first time in 2015 in part due to a number of awareness raising and capacity building activities focused on certified women-owned firms (Rimmer, 2017[12]). The Swiss gender wage transparency certification process requires firms with more than 100 employees to undergo an audit of their wages by gender, and includes random checks of other firms, as a pre-requisite to applying to federal procurement opportunities (OECD, 2021[9]).

www.ingramcontent.com/pod-product-compliance
Lightning Source LLC
Chambersburg PA
CBHW080620270326
41928CB00016B/3141
9789264570306